FUNdamental Goalkeeping

Written by **Karl Dewazien**
Coaching Director, California Youth Soccer Assn. -N.

I will use "HE", in this book, generically to refer to both boys and girls for the sake of brevity.

Karl Dewazien

Fun Soccer Enterprises
2904 Fine Ave.
Clovis, CA 93612

TABLE OF CONTENTS

GENERAL CHARACTERISTICS AND
DEVELOPMENTAL SKILL TEACHING
U.S. DEPT. OF HEALTH AND HUMAN SERVICES OBSERVATION

YEARS OF AGE 6-12	TEEN YEARS	SPECIFIC
GENERAL - Slow years in physical growth - Differ in Motor Development - Difficulty in accepting mistakes. - Lack ability to make quick decisions	- Physical growth is completing still developing socially and emotionally. - Vary widely in physical characterstics: Same age may vary 12 inches in height and 70-80 pounds in weight. - Girls mature earlier.	**6-9 year old** - Learn skills through self-testing · Experiment with skills in a non-competitive setting. · Low-key competition to test skills. · Need sensitive, qualified instructions in the basic skills of games.
PHYSICAL - Developing: - strength - endurance - agility - speed and flexibility.	- Those who mature early have advantage in physical strength. - Those who mature late have advantage in skills which require agility.	**9-12 year old** -Participate in more intensive skill instruction and practices. -Learn combination of skills as they may occur in a game. -Participate in low-key competition in sports of their choice.
TECHNICAL - NO specialized training - Time to learn skills - Use equipment suitable for age and size - Short fun practices	- Be aware they are "beginners" and "learners". - Improving skills begins with "good" practice. - Learn new skills and perfect old ones.	**13+ year old** They are ready for: - Competition in physical activities.
TACTICAL - Learn the skills of compromise and team play. - Learn to improve with fewer players.	- Avoid player comparisons - Easily discouraged Worry about making mistakes - Self-centered	

Reference: "Children and Youth in Action: Physical Activities and Sports". U.S. Government Printing Office, Washington, D.C. Issued 1980.

For Further reading: Fait, Hollis: Physical Education for the Elementary School Child. Chapter Two-The Physical, Social and Intellectual Characteristics of Children., W.B. Saunders Co. c. 1964.

4

GENERAL CHARACTERISTICS AND
DEVELOPMENTAL SKILL TEACHING
Soviet Observations

YEARS OF AGE	7-11	12-14	15+
GENERAL	- big muscles, gross - motor development - concrete thinking	strengthening of muscles and nervous connection, functional disharmony, skill not stable, ability to analyze, abstract thinking	critical analysis, physical training
PHYSICAL TRAINING	- all-around development, (games, relay, acrobatics, soccer etc) - flexibility and agility	all-around development, emphasis on strength and speed	special emphasis on strength and stamina
TECHNICAL	- test times on drills and skills, expose to various game situations - left and right drills	- all game situations - measuring drills and skills	- measure skills and drills at high speeds, accuracy, complex skills
TACTICAL	- development of attention - sight memory - orientation - individual tactics - learning simple combinations	- complex skills - group activities - mastering mechanical aspects of skills (not just doing but also knowing why) - complex individual activities such as fakes and dekes	- individual and group tactics - defensive positions specialized - options of defensive and offensive team play

Taken from: Soviet sports exercise program: The Gold Medal Guide to Physical
Fitness (by) Norman Mac Lean, -Drake Pub. 1976.

5

GENERAL TIME-LINE GROWTH
OF A GOALKEEPER

UNDER SIX
-NO Goalkeepers

UNDER-EIGHT

TECHNIQUE DEVELOPMENT: *Introduction to the Basics:*
1. Ready Position   2. Movement to ball   3. Ground ball save
4. Securing   5. Bowling release.

UNDER-TEN

TECHNIQUE DEVELOPMENT: *More Basics*
-Under 8 techniques should be somewhat developed.
-Introduce: 6. Below waist saves   7. Punt release.

THE PRACTICE SESSION: *Basic Stage*
-No opponents   -Correct repetition   -FUN.

THE GAME: *NO Specializing*
-Rotate all players into keeper position.

UNDER-TWELVE

TECHNIQUE DEVELOPMENT: *Basic and Game Related Stages.*
   –Under 8 & 10 techniques should be highly developed
   –Introduce: 8. Above waist saves.   9. Diving.
                    10. Baseball release.

TACTICAL DEVELOPMENT: *Introduction to the Basics.*
–Positioning and Angle Play.

THE PRACTICE SESSION: *Game Related Stage.*
–Passive opponents   –Correct repetition   –FUN.

THE GAME: *Beginning of Specialization.*
–Train those players with interest and talent.

UNDER-FOURTEEN

TECHNIQUE: *Mastery of all basic techniques.*
TACTICS: *Further instructions as needed.*
THE PRACTICE SESSION: *Introduction of active opponents.*
–Correct repetition   –FUN.
THE GAME: *Carry at least two (2) keepers per team.*

GRADUAL INCREASE OF
KEEPER RESPONSIBILITY

U-8—Modified Goalkeeper Area.

Hands may be used within this area. Confine childrens thinking/training solely to this area.

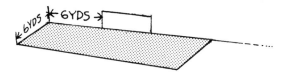

○○

U-12—Increased Modifications

Hands may be used within this area. Confine keepers thinking/training solely to this area.

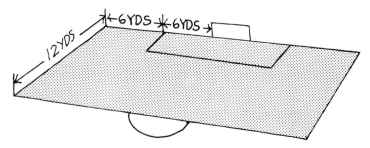

○○

U-14/older—Area increases to F.I.F.A. regulations

Begin training goalkeeper to dominate this area while orchestrating entire field of play.

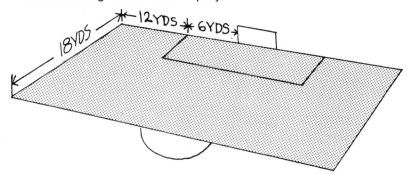

8

ATTRIBUTES ASSOCIATED WITH GOALKEEPING

The keeper position calls for physical and mental skills that a growing child is starting to develop. Being aware of the present stage of development of the individual can aid in the successful training of the keeper. Consider some of the following attributes that are found in the ideal goalkeeper.

PHYSICAL

  1. Height.

Child
current height

Adult
at least 5'9" — 6' 2"

2. **Reflexes:** Able to evaluate the play situation and call upon the muscles required to control the given play.

3. **Flexibility:** Able to Relax—so that entire body is capable of floating in any given direction in response to movement of ball.

4. **Agility:** Able to spring quickly in response to flight of ball.

5. **Mobility:** Having footwork to get quickly off the mark.

6. **Fitness:** Being in top physical condition in order to resist physical challenges.

7. **Strength:** Building durability to meet the specific challenges of this position through organized daily workouts.

ANTICIPATION —

-Reacting to the opponents cue. Having a foreknowledge what the opponents alternatives are and forcing them to do the opposite.

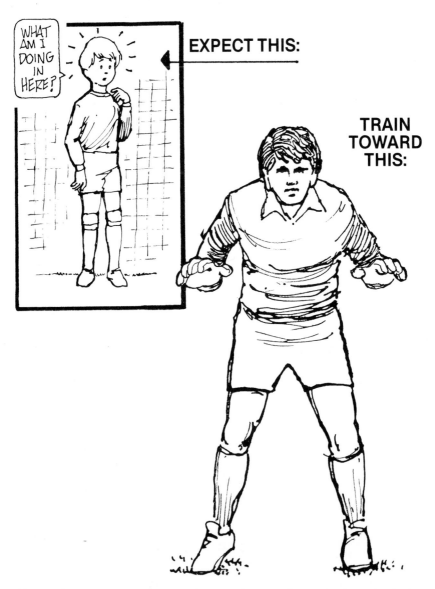

EXPECT THIS:

TRAIN TOWARD THIS:

Young keepers have not had enough experience to know what the opponents choices are...Show them.

CONFIDENCE—Having a strong belief in one's own skills.

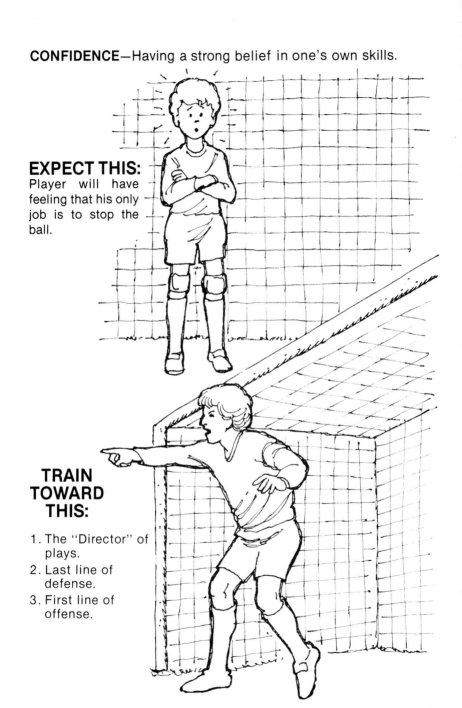

EXPECT THIS:
Player will have feeling that his only job is to stop the ball.

TRAIN TOWARD THIS:

1. The "Director" of plays.
2. Last line of defense.
3. First line of offense.

CONCENTRATION –The ability to control one's thoughts. Directing one's attention to the flow of the game while ignoring distractions from off the field.

EXPECT THIS:

TRAIN TOWARD THIS:

○○

Fact: Most childrens attention span is minimal.

Note: Do not force a child to play in goal just because you feel he belongs there. Have child indicate his desire to play the position and then encourage his development.

COURAGE — Ability to concentrate on the ball while ignoring personal safety.

EXPECT THIS:

TRAIN TOWARD THIS:

Stress the effort your keeper makes rather than the outcome of his actions.

DETERMINATION — Having the mind made up to get the ball –
a firmness of purpose.

EXPECT THIS:

Indecisive with glued down feet.

TRAIN TOWARD THIS:

Hungry for any ball that enters his area.

Note: Emphasize effort and hunger rather than final result while developing the basics.

POSITIONING — The way in which the keeper places himself to the disadvantage of the opponent.

EXPECT THIS:

Feet glued to one spot — generally the goal line.

ⵔⵔⵔⵔⵔⵔⵔⵔⵔⵔⵔⵔⵔⵔⵔⵔⵔⵔⵔⵔⵔⵔⵔⵔⵔⵔⵔⵔⵔⵔⵔⵔⵔⵔⵔⵔⵔⵔ

TRAIN TOWARD THIS:

Cutting off angles – coming off the line.

Note: In training a keeper always begin from a point of reference (goal posts, penalty spot etc.)

15

ORGANIZING THE PRACTICE IN SEVEN STEPS

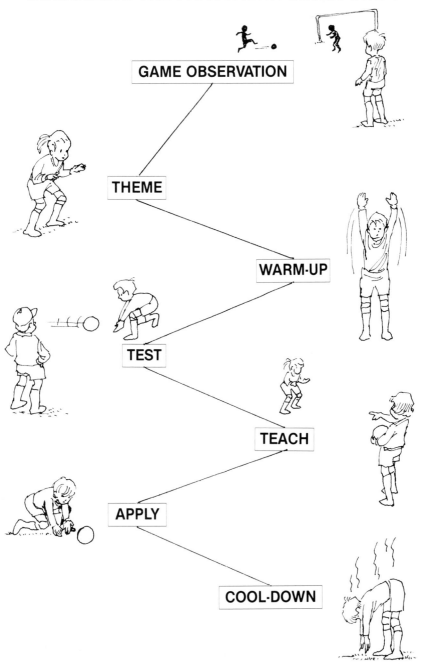

GAME OBSERVATION

THEME

WARM-UP

TEST

TEACH

APPLY

COOL-DOWN

Step 1. **GAME OBSERVATION.**

Take mental or written notes of the most prominent mistakes to be corrected at the next practice.

Be a positive influence for your players during the game.

Step 2. **ESTABLISH THE THEME**

Key on only one technique per practice segment.

Avoid confusing the player with too many topics and instructions.

Step 3. **WARM UP.**

A. **Pre-Stretch.**

Preparing keepers for the rigorous activity of a practice or game is vitally important. Most fitness experts agree that a warm-up is essential for optimal performance and injury prevention. The initial stage should consist of light running or jogging to increase the blood supply to the muscles, increase the rate and force of muscle contractions and raise the body and muscle temperature.

How can you tell when the keepers are ready to stretch?

They should be slightly out of breath and should have broken "the sweat barrrier".

SUGGESTED WARM-UP ROUTINE.

NECK   SHOULDERS   HIPS   BACK

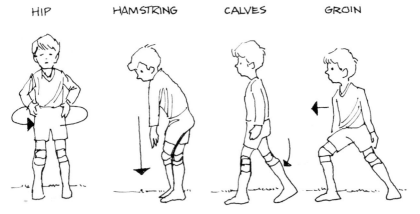

HIP   HAMSTRING   CALVES   GROIN

B. **Stretch.**

For the prevention of injuries, a coach must understand that a player's muscles are surrounded by a sheath of connective tissue called the epimysium. Unless the epimysium is allowed to expand, the muscles will be restricted from a full range of motion, and maximum work capacity from these hindered muscles cannot be expected. Forcing a player to jerk, jump, or run into a state of feeling loose can be harmful, for this procedure may put a hole in the epimysium resulting in a sprain, internal bleeding, or other related muscle injuries. The introduction of a slow deliberate "eight-count" stretching routine is a means toward solving muscle injury problems. These "eight-count" stretching exercises are held to the point where tension is felt and then followed by a brief moment of relaxation. All subsequent movements stretch the muscle group beyond the initial point and continue until the muscle is allowed to stretch to its fullest range of motion. Each exercise is performed for at least one minute per muscle group. But, an entire stretching routine need not last longer than ten minutes to be effective.

STATIC   BOUNCING

19

Step 4. **TESTING.**

Purpose: To convince the keeper of his need to practice the weakness that YOU observed during the last game. YOU must recreate the exact conditions under which the keeper failed to carry out the needed skill.

EXAMPLE:

Your **OBSERVATION:** During the game a consistent weakness was that the legs were spread too wide apart on all ground saves.

Your **THEME:** Improve the leg position on ground saves. (Closing the gap).

Suggested **TEST:** The keeper is to be given 10 serves.

Score card: Out of 10 attempts

SCORE	CONCLUSION	NEED	ACTION
1-3	very poor	Demo/Explain/Practice	FUNdamental Stage
4-5	weak	Demo/Practice	Game related Stage
6-7	good	Practice	Game condition Stage
8-10	excellent	Play	Small sided or Regulation games

NOTE: Avoid comparisons with others. Encourage each keeper to concentrate on self-improvement rather than on keeping up with others.

Step 5. **TEACHING**

Purpose: To eliminate weaknesses and build on the strengths.

PROCEDURE:

Stage 1. Basic (FUNdamental) Stage.

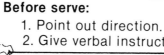

Before serve:
1. Point out direction.
2. Give verbal instruction. (LEFT!)

Stage 2. Game Related Stage.   Increase pace of performance.

Before serve:
Verbal direction (ONLY). (LEFT!)

Stage 3. Game Condition Stage.

Pace of movements (serves – reactions) must resemble the actual game.

Before serve:
No instructions.

Step 6. **APPLICATION**
A. <u>CONTROLLED GAMES</u> (Ruled by the coach).
Alter small sided games in such a way so that a high number of repetitions of the keeper technique to be developed occur.

Helpful Hint:
— Create an atmosphere where the player is allowed to teach himself.
०००

B. <u>FREE GAME</u>. (Controlled by the players). Discipline yourself to know when to leave the keeper alone.

REMEMBER: Over coaching can often be worse than no coaching.

Step 7. **COOL DOWN.**

Many coaches fail to remember the tremendous physical/
mental punishment their keeper must endure during practice
and game situations. The cool-down period must become an
integral part of every coaches training/playing routine.

A. **PHYSICAL COOL-DOWN.**
The PHYSICAL goal is to relieve the tightness created by running and other soccer related activities. Stress on the lower
back is compounded by the unnatural kicking movements
and jarring effects from landing on the solid surface of the
playing field resulting in a narrowing of the spinal vertebrea.
Stretching the spine and opening the narrowed spaces are
necessary. A slow jog and some stretching exercises are sufficient for this training phase.

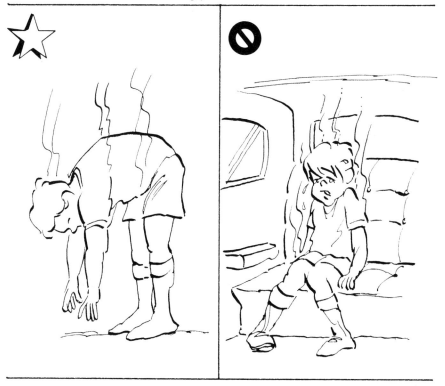

IMPORTANT:
To prevent soreness and injury: Stretches should be done after every
practice and game.

23

B. **MENTAL COOL-DOWN.**

The MENTAL goal is to relieve the tensions created by spectators, peers or personal mistakes. After a practice the keeper must feel prepared for the next game. After a loss a feeling of accomplishment, not failure, must be created. And after a win, keeper must be made aware that more improvement can take place.

Briefly analyze the strong and weak points of their performance.

IMPORTANT:
Coaches must encourage effort, not results.

NOTES FOR BETTER COACHING

1. Try to improve only **ONE** technique at each practice.

2. Provide only **ONE** tip/suggestion on improvement at a time.

3. Encourage questions.

4. Special practices may/should be called for goalkeeper.

5. Special practices should focus on keeper improvement not scorer.

6. If keeper makes an error -- avoid quick or negative criticism.

7. Let the keeper learn from his mistakes after discussion of same.

8. Set reasonable goals based on keeper's ability to grasp and carry-out same.

9. Be patient and he will respect you for it.

10. Hard work and **FUN** are not contradictory in **good** practices!

"Goalkeeping is a difficult position requiring simple skills. What makes great goalkeepers is perfecting these simple skills."

Vincent Lavery

NECESSITIES TO RUN A SUCCESSFUL GOALKEEPER PRACTICE

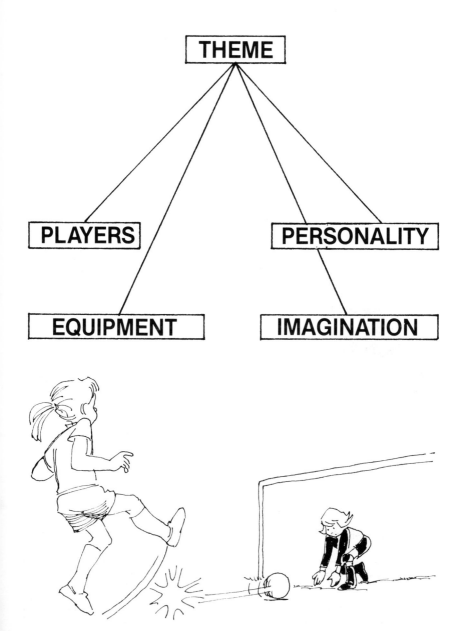

THEME

PLAYERS

PERSONALITY

EQUIPMENT

IMAGINATION

1. PLAYERS — Consider age of players and alter practices accordingly.

TECHNICALLY	
WEAK	**STRONG**
work with the ball	work with and without the ball
MODIFIED GOAL	**REGULATION GOAL**
less field players	more field players

2. **EQUIPMENT:** For Practice

-Goalkeeper jerseys
  —note padding in elbow
-Padded goalkeeper shorts
 (Hip pads)
-Long socks
-Appropriate soccer shoes for
 field conditions
-Towel
-Gloves (optional)
-Tape recording of crowd noise
 from previous game

Suggestions for the game:
   -cap or sun visor (to avoid being dazzled)
   -knee pads. If ground conditions warrant use.
   -extra socks (just in case)
   -extra jersey (avoid color conflict with opponents)
   -various lengths of padded pants (to adjust to field and climate conditions)
   -extra pair of shoes (to adjust to field condition or replacement in case of
    damage)
   -extra pair of shoe laces (just in case)
   -extra pair of gloves (adjust to weather condition)
    NOTE: Gloves should not be skin tight but one size larger than the
    individuals hand size.
   -sweat suit (for warm-up and inclement weather)
   -waterproof bag (to carry towel and other items)

EQUIPMENT (Cont.)

Goals: Sized according to age group.

    a. U-6 and U-8 = 6 ft. high and 6 yds. wide.

    b. U-10 and U-12 = 7 ft. high and 7 yds. wide.

    c. All older age groups = Regulation: 8 ft. high and 8 yds. wide.

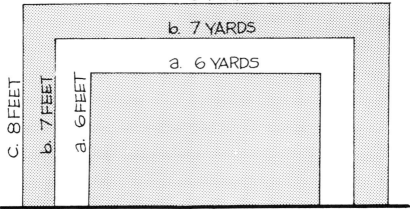

If goal posts are not available you can use:

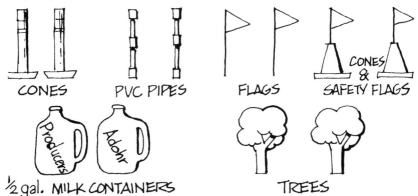

CONES   PVC PIPES   FLAGS   CONES & SAFETY FLAGS

½ gal. MILK CONTAINERS   TREES

* Build substitute goals as close to the real thing as possible (height and width).

●●

C. SOCCER BALLS

Appropriate to each age group:

Size #3   —Under 6 and Under 8 players.

Size #4   —Under 10 and Under 12 players.

Size #5   —All other age groups.

3. **IMAGINATION**

A. **ACTIVITY** — Duplicate the excitement of the game.

B. **REALISM** — Does it happen in the game?
Do not blast stationary ball directly at goal.

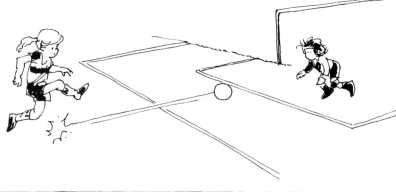

C. **ENJOYMENT** — The genius of good coaching is to make hard work seem like fun.

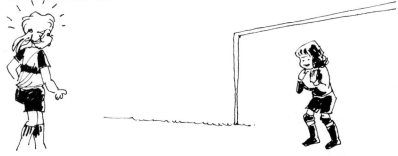

Helpful Hint: Minimize listening and lecture time.
Maximize touches with the ball and playing time.

D. **CHALLENGE and PROGRESSION**

The keeper should be challenged to reach his full potential—resulting in personal satisfaction.

AVOID BEING
TOO SIMPLE—BORED

AVOID BEING
TOO COMPLEX- CONFUSED

BE CREATIVE
—LEARNING

Helpful Hint:

Consider the present skill level of each keeper, then gear exercises and games so that the keeper is challenged.

31

4. PERSONALITY

A. Empathy.

- Learning takes place, resulting from errors made, if the keeper is instructed correctly both verbally and visually.

PARALYSIS through ANALYSIS

Helpful Hint: Coaches should turn keeper error into a positive situation.

⦿⦿

B. Improvement.

POSITIVE REINFORCEMENT

Helpful Hints:

- When improvement does not take place immediately the keeper will not sense failure unless you show a negative reaction.

- With patience and encouragement children will progress on and off the soccer field.

> • Understand - they are "Learners".

PATIENCE. You must not expect immediate results.

PERSISTENCE. It will take time and effective repetition.

FLEXIBILITY. To maintain player interest when working on a particular technique.

SENSE OF HUMOR. The player should work in a relaxed atmosphere.

MOST IMPORTANT

BE YOURSELF!

REMEMBER: Construct game environment during practice sessions thus avoiding surprises for match play.

THE LEARNING STAGES FOR THE GOALKEEPER

OBSERVATION

Watch advanced keepers practice and play.

COACH

– Give demonstrations slowly, simply and technically correct.

IMITATION

Try to re-enact the technique observed.

Stages of Progression: From slow to faster performance.

PRACTICE

Improve and polish the technique so that IT becomes instinctive.

Stages of Progression: From FUNdamental to Game Condition

PLAY

Perform the technique during the game.

Stages of Progression: From Small-Sided Games to Regulation Game.

THE SEVEN-STEP APPROACH FOR TEACHING THE GOALKEEPER

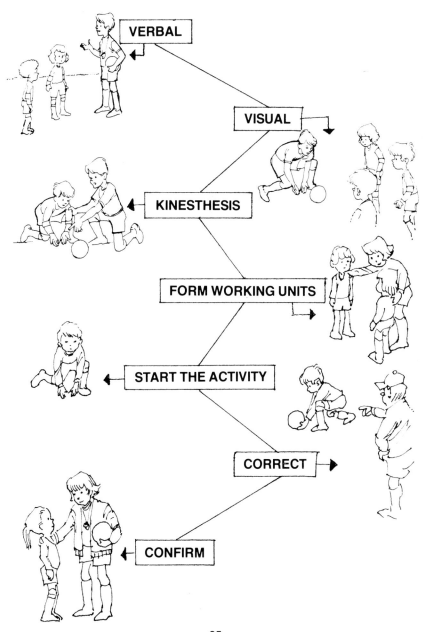

VERBAL

VISUAL

KINESTHESIS

FORM WORKING UNITS

START THE ACTIVITY

CORRECT

CONFIRM

Step 1.   Use the spoken word as a teaching tool.
VERBAL

I HEAR AND I FORGET

For SUCCESS .... Be clear, concise and brief.
●●
Step 2.

VISUAL Utilize pictures, motion pictures or
demonstrations as a teaching tool.

I SEE AND I REMEMBER

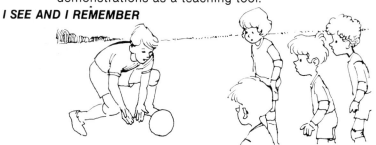

For SUCCESS .... Be slow, correct and brief.
●●
Step 3.

KINESTHESIS Physically adjust the keepers body to help
achieve the correct form through a realization of
how it "feels".

*I DO AND
I UNDERSTAND*

For SUCCESS...Assist in several repetitions so the keeper will
get the "feel" of the correct movement.

36

Step 4. **FORM WORKING UNITS**

Be creative – Create an environment which forces the keeper to make decisions and learn on his own.

Some Examples:

1. One Keeper (Ball)

2. One Keeper (Ball & Wall)

3. Two Keepers (Ball)

4. Two Keepers (Ball & Wall)

5. Three Keepers (Ball)

NOTE: It is highly recommended that the keepers practice their basic techniques in front of a goal.

Step 5. **START THE ACTIVITY** – Three Stages:
1. Basic (FUNdamental).
2. Game Related.
3. Game Condition

Stage 1. **BASIC** (FUNdamental) **STAGE**
Create an atmosphere in which the keeper can experiment with his natural abilities so he may experience his strengths and weaknesses. Take into consideration:

The Serve — Easy hand release toward harder hand release.

Distance — Further away – giving time to react correctly.

Instructions — Point out and call out the direction of the coming serve.

Time between serves — Long — allowing physical and mental recovery.

PRACTICAL APPLICATION: Straight Serve.

Step 5. Continued:

        Increase pace of performance.

The Serve—Hard hand release toward easy foot release.

Distance—Closer - still allowing for reaction time.

Instructions—Call out directions of coming serve.

Time between serves—Shorter-look for physical recovery.

PRACTICAL APPLICATION: Reachable Serve:

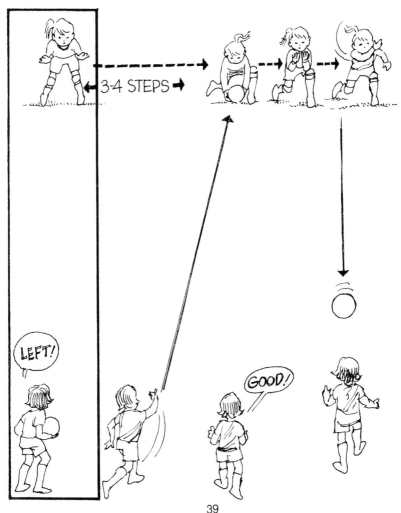

Step 5. Continued:

Stage 3. **GAME CONDITION STAGE.**
 Pace of movements (serves – reactions) must
 resemble the actual game.

The Serve—From soft to hard shots on goal.

Distance—Varies according to goalkeeper needs.

Instructions—Are eliminated.

Time between serves—Depends on goalkeeper fitness and abilities.

PRACTICAL APPLICATION: Challenging Serve.

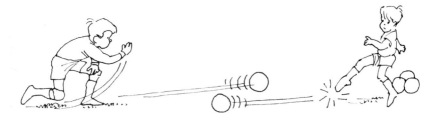

NOTE: The goals of a practice are to improve technique and avoid
 fatigue.

40

Step 6. **CORRECT.** Consistent basic faults should be corrected through guided questioning and repetition of movement.

FOR EXAMPLE: The Coach is discussing the **SEMI-KNEEL SAVE.**

Consistent Mistake:

Barrier Knee Touching the Ground

Coaches Question:

Should the Barrier Knee Touch the Ground?

Keepers Answer

Right		Wrong
Positive statement by the coach.		Coach repeat. Demo/Explanation
Coach encourages correct repetition.		Keeper imitates coaches example.

Step 7. **CONFIRM.** End the practice with a critique of what has taken place.

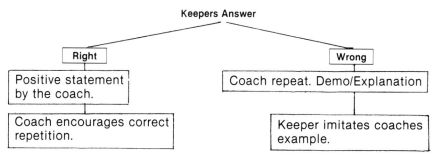

41

THEME: "READY POSITION"

All defensive moves by the goalkeeper are initiated from the "ready position". This position should be instinctively assumed whenever the opponents are within shooting distance.

What is the "ready position"? The "ready position" requires that:

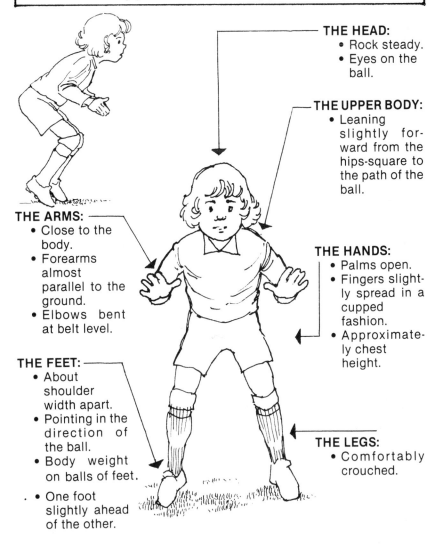

THE HEAD:
- Rock steady.
- Eyes on the ball.

THE UPPER BODY:
- Leaning slightly forward from the hips-square to the path of the ball.

THE ARMS:
- Close to the body.
- Forearms almost parallel to the ground.
- Elbows bent at belt level.

THE HANDS:
- Palms open.
- Fingers slightly spread in a cupped fashion.
- Approximately chest height.

THE FEET:
- About shoulder width apart.
- Pointing in the direction of the ball.
- Body weight on balls of feet.
- One foot slightly ahead of the other.

THE LEGS:
- Comfortably crouched.

SUMMARY: The above directions should be followed instinctively whenever a dangerous situation develops which may result in a shot on goal.

READY POSITION — Common Faults

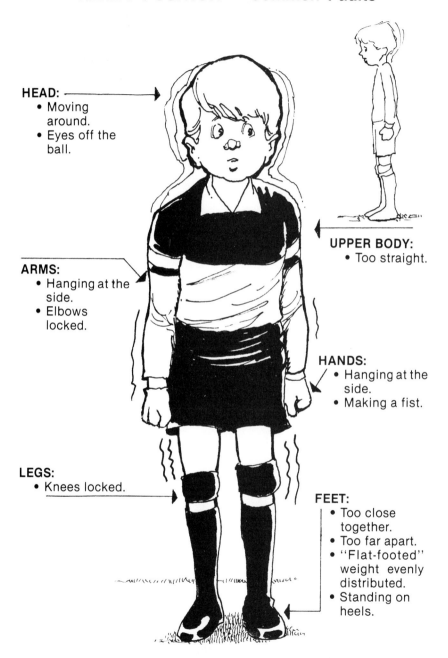

HEAD:
- Moving around.
- Eyes off the ball.

UPPER BODY:
- Too straight.

ARMS:
- Hanging at the side.
- Elbows locked.

HANDS:
- Hanging at the side.
- Making a fist.

LEGS:
- Knees locked.

FEET:
- Too close together.
- Too far apart.
- "Flat-footed" weight evenly distributed.
- Standing on heels.

GETTING INTO "READY POSITION"

1. Verbal command:

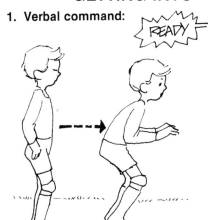

Step 1. Goalkeeper stands erect with eyes closed.
Step 2. Coach gives verbal signal "ready".
Step 3. Goalkeeper assumes "ready position" as quickly as possible.

CHALLENGE: Coach calls other instructions — Goalkeeper reacts only on hearing "ready".

2. Sound signal:

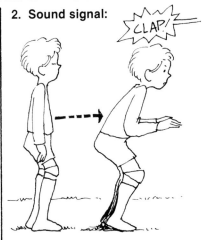

Step 1. Goalkeeper stands erect with eyes closed.
Step 2. Coach gives sound signal (example: clap of hands).
Step 3. Goalkeeper assumes "ready position" as quickly as possible.

CHALLENGE: Coach makes other sounds (whistle, snap of fingers, etc.). Goalkeeper is to react only to the agreed sound.

3. Physical signal:

Step 1. Goalkeeper stands erect.
Step 2. Coach gives visual signal (example: movement of right leg).
Step 3. Goalkeeper assumes "ready position" as quickly as possible.

CHALLENGE: Coach gives other movements (ex: lifting arm). Goalkeeper is to react only to agreed movement.

4. Goalkeeper in motion:

Step 1. Goalkeeper is walking forward.
Step 2. Coach gives a "signal".
Step 3. Goalkeeper assumes "ready position" as quickly as possible.

CHALLENGE: Increase speed of movement by Goalkeeper (jog, run, sprint).

GETTING "READY" FROM AWKWARD POSITIONS.

1. Turning:

Step 1. Goalkeeper faces away from the coach.
Step 2. Coach gives a prearranged "signal".
Step 3. Goalkeeper turns as quickly as possible and assumes proper "ready position" facing coach.

CHALLENGE: Placing several balls in eighteen yard penalty area. Goalkeeper assumes "ready position" facing a certain ball.

2. From kneeling position:

Step 1. Give a pre-arranged signal.
Step 2. Goalkeeper stands up as quickly as possible in "ready position".

3. From prone position:

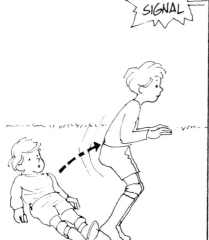

Step 1. Give a pre-arranged signal
Step 2. Goalkeeper get up as quickly as possible in "ready position".

4. After an exercise.

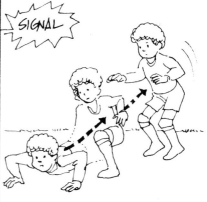

Step 1. Do a pre-arranged exercise (example: push-up).
Step 2. Recover as quickly as possible.
Step 3. Assume a proper "ready position".

CHALLENGE: Progress from simple exercises to more difficult.

STAYING IN "READY POSITION"

1. Shuffle right and left (Correctly).

Shuffle right and left (Incorrectly).

Do not cross legs.

Crossing the legs.

Key: Keep the head "rock steady".

3. Moving forward and backward (Correctly).

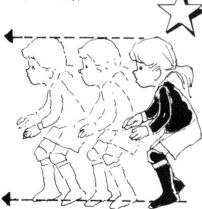

4. Moving forward and backward (Incorrectly).

Head stays at the same height — "rock steady".

Head going up and down with each step.

RECOMMENDATION: Do not introduce a ball to Keeper exercises until the "Ready Position" is learned.

THEME: Receiving a Rolling Ball:

Two of the more popular means in stopping rolling/ground balls are the "Semi-Kneel" and the "Standing Save". Allow each keeper to bring their personal approach to performing these two techniques. Keep in mind some of the following basics:

SEMI-KNEEL SAVE

UPPER BODY – In line with the rolling ball, twisted at the waist and leaning forward.

PLANT LEG — Knee flexed and pointing away from path of ball.

THE ARMS – *Lowered* and reaching for the ball

FINGERS — Spread with pinkies touching (forming M), nails lightly touching the ground.

BARRIER LEG – Bent knee does not touch the ground.
–Knee close to the ankle of the plant foot.

THE HANDS (First Barrier) – Cupped in line with the rolling ball, moving to scoop it up.

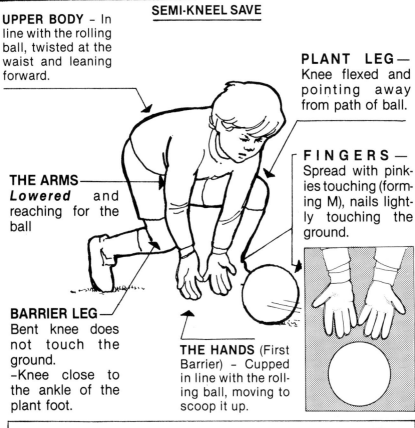

Note: Ball coming right side—**right leg** becomes **plant leg.**
Ball coming from left side—**left leg** becomes **plant leg.**

48

SEMI-KNEEL SAVE
Common faults:

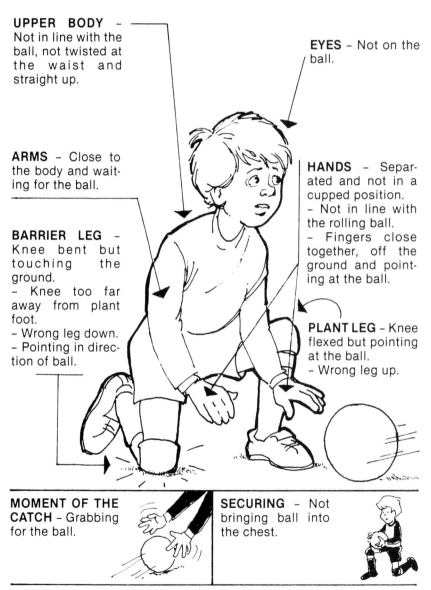

UPPER BODY – Not in line with the ball, not twisted at the waist and straight up.

EYES – Not on the ball.

ARMS – Close to the body and waiting for the ball.

HANDS – Separated and not in a cupped position.
– Not in line with the rolling ball.
– Fingers close together, off the ground and pointing at the ball.

BARRIER LEG – Knee bent but touching the ground.
– Knee too far away from plant foot.
– Wrong leg down.
– Pointing in direction of ball.

PLANT LEG – Knee flexed but pointing at the ball.
– Wrong leg up.

MOMENT OF THE CATCH – Grabbing for the ball.

SECURING – Not bringing ball into the chest.

SUMMARY:
- Moving into the path of the ball too slowly.
- Not bringing the hands behind the ball.
- Not bringing the legs behind the hands.

TESTING "SEMI-KNEEL SAVE"

Purpose:
To see how proficient the keeper is· in performing "Semi-Kneel Saves" and what time and instruction is needed to perfect this skill.

Suggested Test:
Ten serves to right and ten serves to left side.

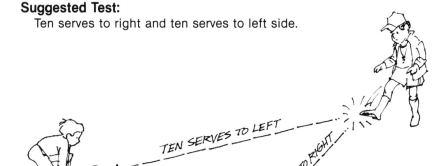

Rating:
Observe the technique in its component parts–

1. Plant leg
2. Barrier leg
3. Upper body action
4. Hand action
5. Arm action
6. Ball action

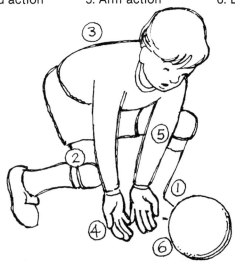

NOTE: Get hands behind the ball—and body behind the hands.

"SEMI-KNEEL SAVE" TRAINING.

Exercise 1. Stationary Ball.

    a . The scoop.
        –From the "Ready Position" take one step to scoop-up ball using correct "Semi-Kneel" technique.

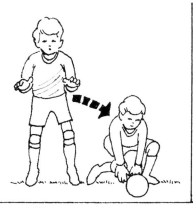 

b. The Shuffle
–Shuffling from right and left sides, in "Ready Position", move to scoop-up stationary ball using correct "Semi-Kneel" technique.

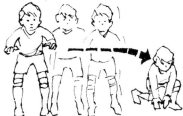

c. Moving forward
–Move forward in "Ready Position".
–Then move to scoop-up stationary ball using correct "Semi-Kneel" technique.

SEMI-KNEEL TRAINING (Continued)

Keeper works with Ball and Wall.

Exercise 1. Keeper uses **two-handed serve** off wall–Then approaches ball and applies correct "Semi-Kneel" technique in gathering ball.

Exercise 2. Keeper uses **one-handed serve** off wall–

Exercise 3. Keeper uses **push pass serve** off wall–

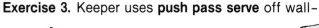

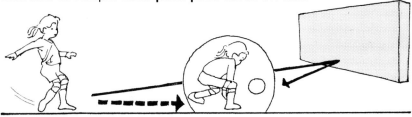

Exercise 4. Keeper uses **instep kick serve** off wall–

Approach:

SEMI-KNEEL TRAINING (Continued)

Exercise 5. Keeper uses **two handed hike** off wall–Then turns 180° and uses correct "Semi-Kneel" technique in gathering ball.

Exercise 6. Keeper uses **one handed hike** off wall–

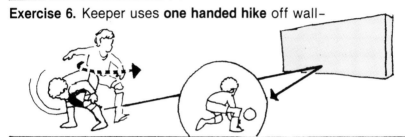

Exercise 7. Keeper uses **push pass serve** off wall–Then does an exercise (Ex: sit down) to be followed by the "Semi-Kneel" save.

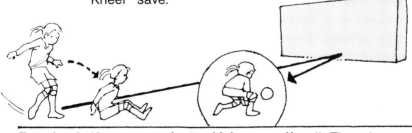

Exercise 8. Keeper uses **instep kick serve** off wall–Then does an exercise (Ex: push up) to be followed by the "Semi-Kneel" save.

SEMI-KNEEL TRAINING (Continued)
TWO-KEEPERS USING BALL and WALL.

Exercise 1. Assistant uses **"Bowling" serve** off wall–Keeper faces the wall in "Ready Position" and gathers ricochet with "Semi-Kneel" technique.

○○○

Exercise 2. Assistant uses **Push pass** **serve** off wall–

○○

Exercise 3. Assistant uses **Instep kick** serve off wall–

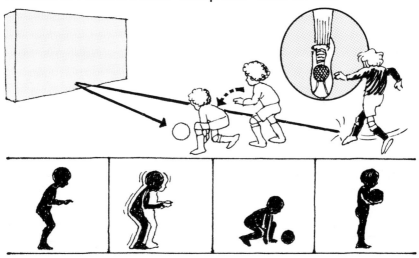

SEMI-KNEEL TRAINING (Continued)

4. Variety may be added to the preceding exercises by using the following serves:
   a. Ball served to:

Right side of keeper only.

Left side of keeper only.

Between keeper legs.

   b. Balls served at varying angles:

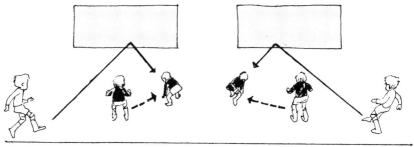

   c. Keeper faces assistant who serves ball off wall – Forcing keeper to make 180° turn to collect ball.

NOTES: Increase the distance from wall and decrease speed of serve with beginning players—Reverse as keeper improves.

A wall may be used as a partner for all keeper drills involving saves and ball distribution. Be creative.

STANDING SAVE
"The Bow"

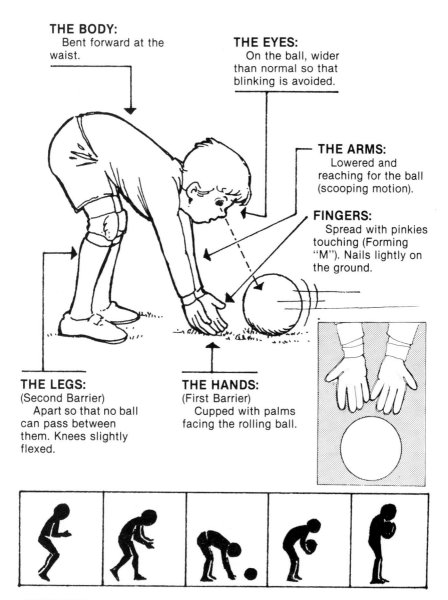

THE BODY:
Bent forward at the waist.

THE EYES:
On the ball, wider than normal so that blinking is avoided.

THE ARMS:
Lowered and reaching for the ball (scooping motion).

FINGERS:
Spread with pinkies touching (Forming "M"). Nails lightly on the ground.

THE LEGS:
(Second Barrier)
Apart so that no ball can pass between them. Knees slightly flexed.

THE HANDS:
(First Barrier)
Cupped with palms facing the rolling ball.

SUMMARY: Move into the path of the ball quickly.
Bring both hands behind the ball.
Bring both feet behind the hands for safety.
Important: Let the ball roll into the hands.

STANDING SAVE
Common Faults:

THE BODY:
Too straight.

EYES:
Not on the ball.

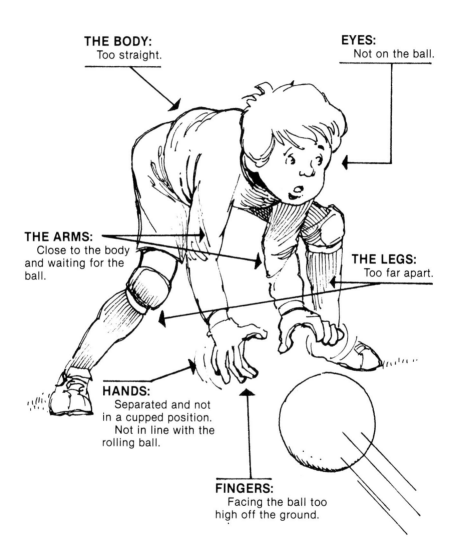

THE ARMS:
Close to the body and waiting for the ball.

THE LEGS:
Too far apart.

HANDS:
Separated and not in a cupped position. Not in line with the rolling ball.

FINGERS:
Facing the ball too high off the ground.

SUMMARY OF MISTAKES:
- Moving into the path of the ball too slowly.
- Not bringing the hands behind the ball.
- Not bringing the feet behind the hands.
- **Most common:** Grabbing for the ball.

57

TESTING "STANDING SAVE" TECHNIQUE

Purpose:

To see how proficient the keeper is in performing "Standing Saves" and what time and instruction is needed to perfect this skill.

Suggested Test:

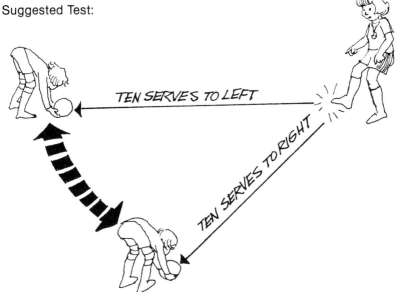

TEN SERVES TO LEFT

TEN SERVES TO RIGHT

Rating:

Observe the technique in its component parts —

1. Leg action   2. Hand action   3. Arm action
4. Body action   5. Head action   6. Ball action

"STANDING SAVE" TRAINING

Exercise 1. STATIONARY BALL

a. The scoop.
   Step 1. "Ready Position".
   Step 2. Reach to scoop-up stationary ball using correct "Standing Save" technique.

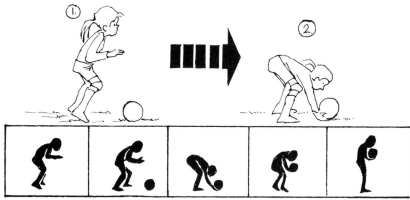

b. The shuffle.
   Step 1. "Ready Position".
   Step 2. Shuffle from right and left sides to scoop-up ball.

c. Moving forward.
   Step 1. Move forward in "Ready Position".
   Step 2. Scoop-up stationary ball.

STANDING SAVE TRAINING (Continued).

TWO KEEPERS and BALL

Roll ball to partner.
Step 1. "Ready Position". Step 2. Approach ball.
Step 3. Reach to scoop up ball. Step 4. "Secure" ball.
Step 5. Roll ball back to partner.

Roll ball to **right** and **left** of partner.
Step 1. "Ready Position". Step 2. Shuffle sideways into path of ball.
Repeat steps 3, 4 and 5.

Roll ball **short** of partner.
Step 1. "Ready Position". Step 2. Move Forward.
Repeat steps 3, 4 and 5.

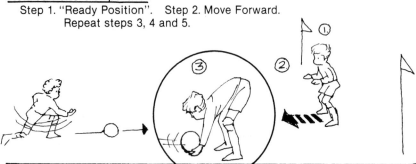

STANDING SAVE TRAINING (Continued).

Push pass ball to partner.
Step 1. "Ready Position".   Step 2. Approach ball.
Repeat steps 3, 4 and 5.

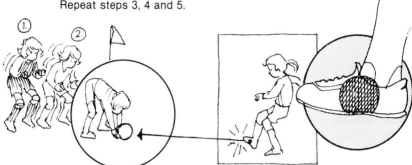

ⓞⓞⓞⓞⓞⓞⓞⓞⓞⓞⓞⓞⓞⓞⓞⓞⓞⓞⓞⓞⓞⓞⓞⓞⓞⓞ ⓞⓞⓞⓞⓞⓞⓞⓞⓞⓞⓞⓞⓞⓞⓞⓞⓞⓞⓞⓞⓞⓞ

Push pass ball to **right** and **left** of partner.
Step 1. "Ready Position".   Step 2. Shuffle sideways into path of ball.
Repeat steps 3, 4 and 5.

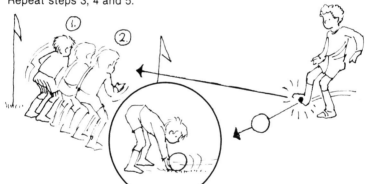

ⓞⓞⓞ

Push pass ball **short** of partner.
Step 1. "Ready Position".   Step 2. Move Forward.
Repeat steps 3, 4 and 5.

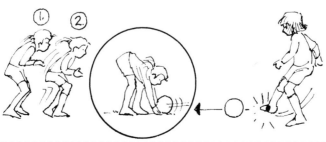

ⓞⓞⓞ

STANDING SAVE TRAINING (Continued).

Turn then Save.
Step 1. Face away from partner in "Ready Position".
Step 2. Listen for verbal signal.
Step 3. Turn quickly on given signal.
Step 4. Approach and scoop-up ball.
Step 5. "Secure" ball and repeat sequence.

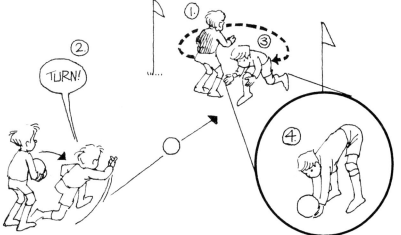

Turn to right or left.
Step 1. Face away from partner in "Ready Position".
Step 2. Listen for verbal signal.
Step 3. **Turn** quickly **in direction called** ("left" or "right").
Repeat steps 4 and 5.

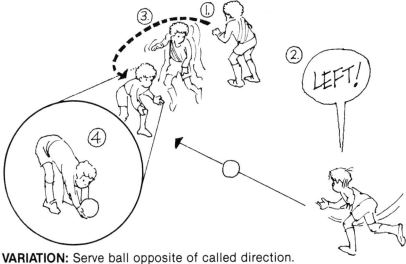

VARIATION: Serve ball opposite of called direction.

62

STANDING SAVE TRAINING (Continued).

One hand hike and save.

Step 1. Hike ball between the legs (one hand only).
Step 2. Turn and recover into "Ready Position".
Step 3. Approach and scoop-up ball.
Step 4. "Secure" ball and repeat sequence.

oooooooooooooooooooooooooooooooooooooooooooooooooooooooooooooo

Two handed hike and save.

Step 1. Hike ball between the legs (use both hands).
Repeat steps 2, 3, 4 and 5.

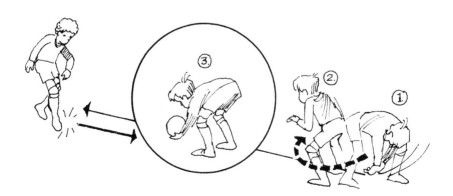

oooooooooooooooooooooooooooooooooooooooooooooooooooooooooooo

STANDING SAVE TRAINING (Continued).

Shuffle-**roll**-save.
Step 1. One keeper with ball—partner in "Ready Position".
Step 2. Shuffle sideways together.
Step 3. Alternate rolling and saving the ball.
Step 4. "Secure" ball and repeat sequence.

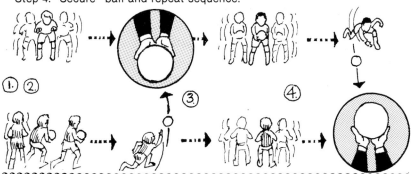

Shuffle-**lead roll**-save.
Step 1 and 2. Same as above.
Step 3. Alternate rolling ball beyond partners position.

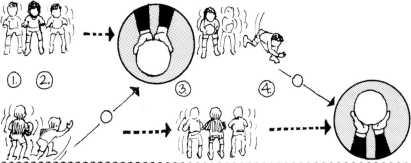

One **forward** One **backward.**
Step 1. Same as above.
Step 2. One moves forward one moves backward.
Step 3. Alternate rolling and saving the ball.

STANDING SAVE TRAINING (Continued).
Shuffle-**push pass**-save.
   Step 1. One keeper with ball—partner in "Ready Position".
   Step 2. Shuffle sideways together.
   Step 3. Alternate passing and saving the ball.

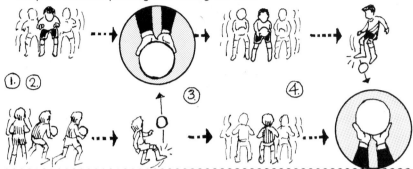

Shuffle-**lead pass**-save.
   Step 1 and 2. Same as above.
   Step 3. Alternate passing ball beyond partners position.

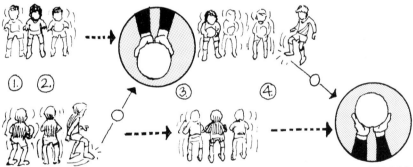

One **forward** One **backward**.
   Step 1. Same as above.
   Step 2. One moves forward one moves backward.
   Step 3. Alternate passing and saving the ball.

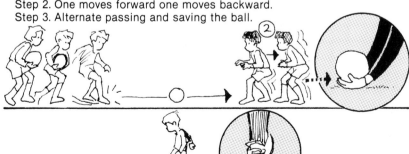

Variation: **Instep pass** ball to partner.

STANDING SAVE TRAINING (Continued).

Awkward positions.
Step 1. Awkward position (Example: kneeling).
Step 2. Move quickly into "Ready Position".
Step 3. Approach and scoop-up ball.
Step 4. "Secure" ball and repeat sequence.

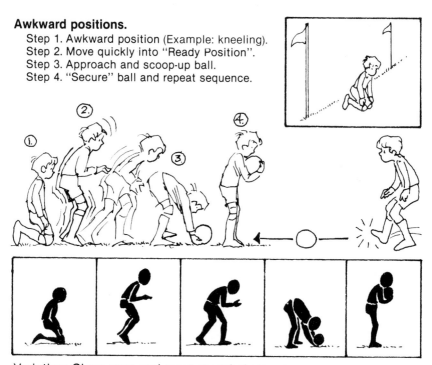

Variation: Close eyes and react at verbal signal.

○○

Exercise then Save.
Step 1. Execute given exercise (Example: Forward roll).
Repeat steps 2, 3, 4 and 5.

○○

STANDING SAVE TRAINING (Continued).

TWO KEEPERS and TWO BALLS.

Simultaneous **roll.**

    Step 1. Stand across from partner. Step 2. Roll ball to partner.
Step 3. Approach and collect oncoming ball.

Simultaneous **side** roll.

    Step 1. Stand across from partner. Step 2. Roll ball to **right** or **left** of partner.
Step 3. Approach and collect oncoming ball.

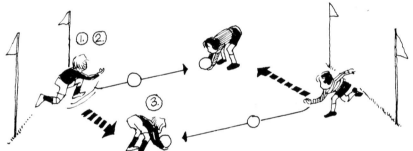

Simultaneous **straight** roll.

    Step 1. Stand at a diagonal from partner. Step 2. Roll ball straight ahead.
Step 3. Shuffle to collect partner's ball.

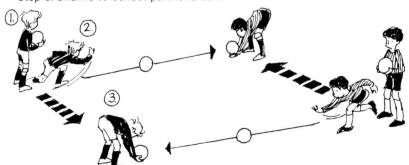

MEDIUM HEIGHT BALLS
(Below the Waist)

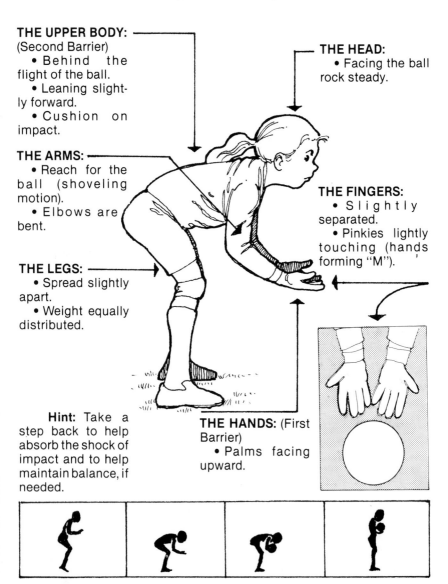

THE UPPER BODY:
(Second Barrier)
- Behind the flight of the ball.
- Leaning slightly forward.
- Cushion on impact.

THE ARMS:
- Reach for the ball (shoveling motion).
- Elbows are bent.

THE LEGS:
- Spread slightly apart.
- Weight equally distributed.

THE HEAD:
- Facing the ball rock steady.

THE FINGERS:
- Slightly separated.
- Pinkies lightly touching (hands forming "M").

Hint: Take a step back to help absorb the shock of impact and to help maintain balance, if needed.

THE HANDS: (First Barrier)
- Palms facing upward.

SUMMARY:
- Move quickly forward to meet the ball.
- Meet the ball with hands, then arms and then the body.
- Bring body behind the hands for safety.

MEDIUM HEIGHT SAVES
Common Faults

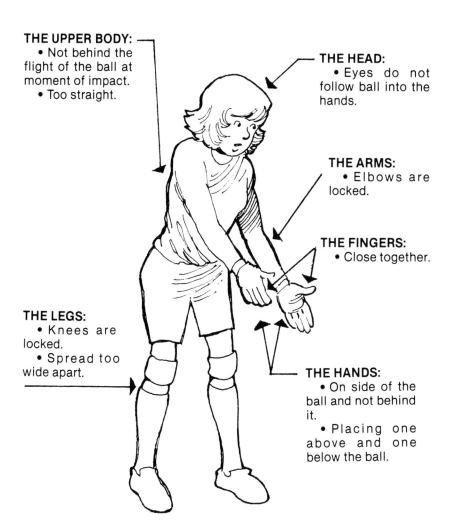

THE UPPER BODY:
• Not behind the flight of the ball at moment of impact.
• Too straight.

THE HEAD:
• Eyes do not follow ball into the hands.

THE ARMS:
• Elbows are locked.

THE FINGERS:
• Close together.

THE LEGS:
• Knees are locked.
• Spread too wide apart.

THE HANDS:
• On side of the ball and not behind it.
• Placing one above and one below the ball.

MOST COMMON MISTAKES:

• Palms make first contact with ball rather than fingers.

• Meeting the ball with body first.

• Crossing one leg over the other while attempting to get body behind the flight of the ball.

69

TESTING "BELOW WAIST SAVE" TECHNIQUE

Purpose:

To see how proficient goalkeeper is in making "Below Waist Saves" and what time and instructions are needed to perfect this skill.

Suggested Test:

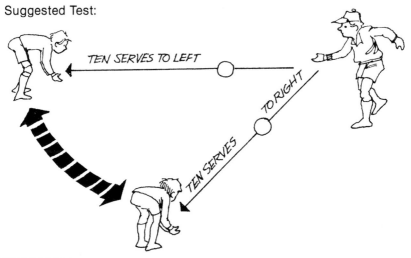

Rating:

Observe the technique in its component parts—

1. Head action   2. Body action   3. Arm action
4. Hand action   5. Leg action   6. Feet action
7. Ball action

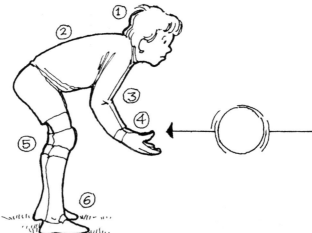

Note: Do not teach through fear or pain—start with slow and accurate serves to build keepers confidence.

"BELOW THE WAIST" SAVE (Training notes):

Type of Serve:
    Beginning   —Underhand tosses (only).
    Intermediate   —Underhand and overhand tosses.
    Advanced   —Combination of above plus instep kick.

Height of Serve:
    Beginning   —Consistent and accurate to hands.
    Intermediate   —From knees to belly button.
    Advanced   —From ankles to chest.

Speed of Serve:
    Beginning   —Slow to build confidence.
    Intermediate   —Challenging.
    Advanced   —Game condition.

Number of Repetitions:
    Beginning   —Ten saves   — One minute rest.
    Intermediate   —Thirty saves   — One minute rest.
    Advanced   —Forty-five seconds
                          work   — One minute rest.

IMPORTANT: Confidence building must be the first procedure in teaching "below the waist" saves. The distance of the toss can eliminate some of the fears (short at first then increase distance with technique development).

"BELOW WAIST SAVE" TRAINING.

Stationary ball. Ball held below waist height by partner.
  —From "Ready position" use correct technique in taking ball.

①  ②

Simulated flight. Ball transferred into keeper's waiting hands from partner's hands.
  —From "Ready position" use correct technique in collecting handed-over ball.

①  ②

Accurate underhand toss.
  —From "Ready position" use correct technique in catching tossed ball.

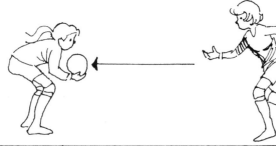

"BELOW WAIST SAVE" TRAINING (Continued).

Clasp hands in front.
Step 1. Face partner with hands clasped (front).
Step 2. Make appropriate moves to collect oncoming ball.
Step 3. Return ball and continue sequence.

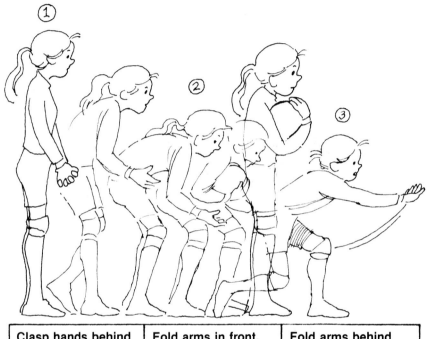

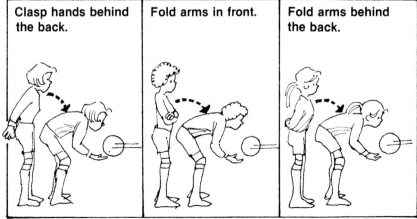

Clasp hands behind the back.	Fold arms in front.	Fold arms behind the back.

VARIATION:
Start these exercises with keeper's eyes closed and add verbal signal.

"BELOW THE WAIST SAVE" TRAINING (Continued).
THREE-KEEPERS and BALL.

Shuffle—catch—shuffle.
    Step 1. Goaltender in "Ready Position".
    Step 2. Shuffle left and catch ball using proper technique.
    Step 3. Return ball to third keeper.
    Step 4. Shuffle right and repeat sequence.

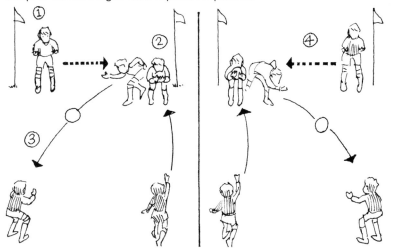

Shuffle—catch—turn and shuffle.
    Steps 1. 2. Same as above.
    Step 3. Turn 180° and toss ball to third keeper.
    Step 4. Shuffle left and repeat sequence.

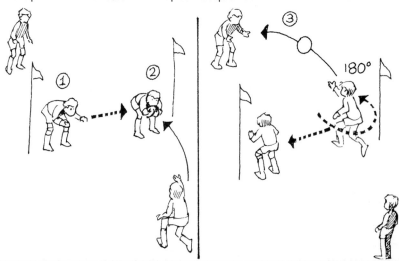

"BELOW THE WAIST SAVE" TRAINING (Continued).
THREE-KEEPERS and BALL.

Catch the toss—turn—and toss.

Step 1. Toss ball to goaltender.
Step 2. Goaltender—catch ball using proper technique.
Step 3. Turn and toss ball to third keeper.
Step 4. Repeat sequence in opposite direction.

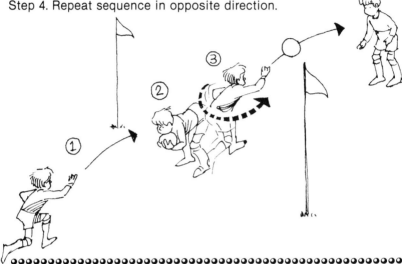

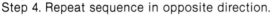

Catch the toss—turn—catch the volley kick.

Step 1. 2. 3. Same as above.
Step 4. Third keeper—return ball to middle with volley kick.
Step 5. Repeat sequence.

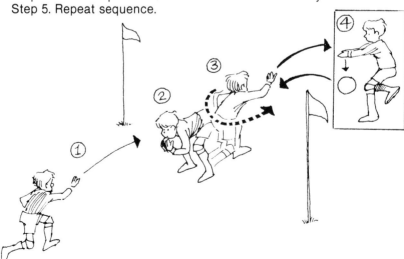

"BELOW THE WAIST SAVE" TRAINING (Continued).
THREE-KEEPERS two BALLS.

Catch the toss—turn—catch the toss.
Step 1. Toss ball to goaltender.
Step 2. Catch ball using proper technique.
Step 3. Return ball to server.
Step 4. Turn 180°and prepare for serve from third keeper.
Step 5. Continue sequence from opposite direction.

Catch the toss—turn—catch the volley kick.
Steps 1. 2. 3. 4. Same as above.
Step 5. Third keeper—volley kick ball at goaltender.
Step 6. Catch ball and return to third keeper.
Step 7. Turn 180°and repeat sequence.

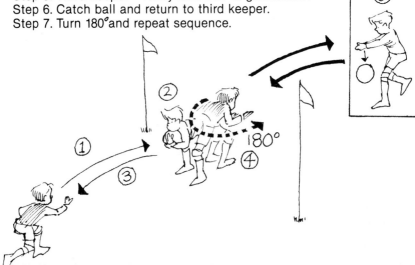

"BELOW THE WAIST SAVE" TRAINING (Continued).
THREE-KEEPERS two BALLS.

After an exercise.
   Step 1. Goaltender in "Ready Position."
   Step 2. Execute given exercise (Example: Push-up)
   Step 3. Prepare and catch the ball.
   Step 4. Return ball to server.
   Step 5. Turn 180° and repeat the sequence.

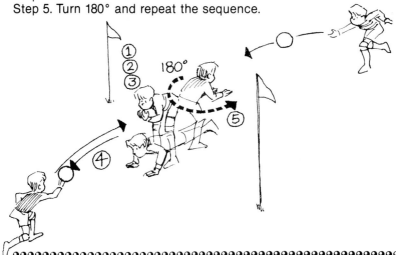

Over an obstacle.
   Step 1. Jump over an obstacle in "Ready Position."
   Step 2. Prepare and catch the ball.
   Step 3. Return ball to server.
   Step 4. Turn 180° and repeat sequence.

HIGH BALL SAVES
(Above the Waist)

Once the keeper has decided to catch the ball - total concentration and eyes must be directed to ball. He must then time his movement toward the ball (judgment) so as to receive it as high as possible, with both hands. Again, the technique required is extremely individualistic but should involve some of the following basics:

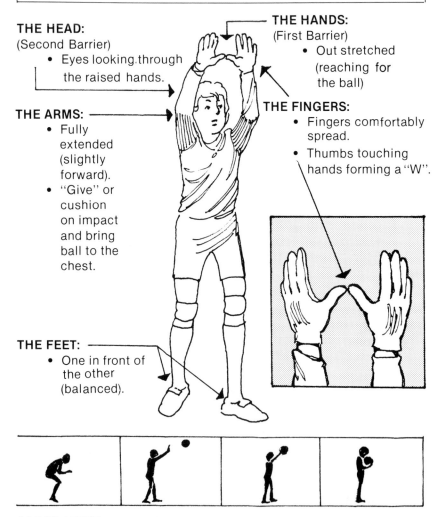

THE HEAD:
(Second Barrier)
- Eyes looking through the raised hands.

THE ARMS:
- Fully extended (slightly forward).
- "Give" or cushion on impact and bring ball to the chest.

THE FEET:
- One in front of the other (balanced).

THE HANDS:
(First Barrier)
- Out stretched (reaching for the ball)

THE FINGERS:
- Fingers comfortably spread.
- Thumbs touching hands forming a "W".

ADDED HINTS:
- Let teammates know that your are ready to catch the ball (verbal communication).
- IF POSSIBLE NEVER LET A BALL BOUNCE

HIGH BALL SAVES
Common Faults

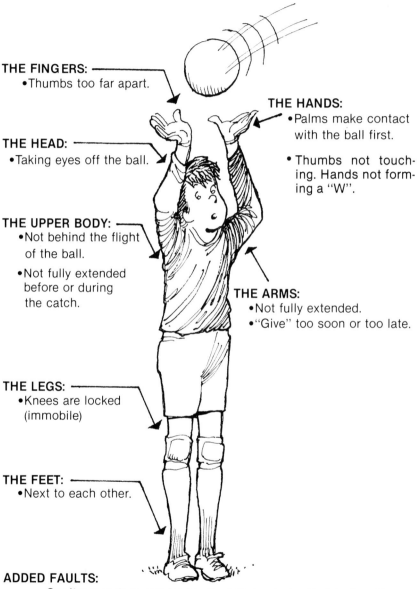

THE FINGERS: ───────
- Thumbs too far apart.

THE HANDS:
- Palms make contact with the ball first.
- Thumbs not touching. Hands not forming a "W".

THE HEAD: ───────
- Taking eyes off the ball.

THE UPPER BODY: ───
- Not behind the flight of the ball.
- Not fully extended before or during the catch.

THE ARMS:
- Not fully extended.
- "Give" too soon or too late.

THE LEGS: ───────
- Knees are locked (immobile)

THE FEET: ───────
- Next to each other.

ADDED FAULTS:
- Goalkeeper does not let his teammates know that he is going for the high ball. (Verbally)
- Letting the ball bounce.

TESTING "ABOVE WAIST SAVE" TECHNIQUE

Purpose:

   To see how proficient goalkeeper is in making "Above Waist Saves" and what time and instructions are needed to perfect this skill.

Suggested Test:

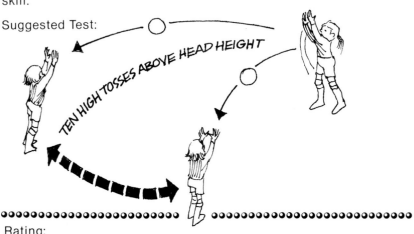

TEN HIGH TOSSES ABOVE HEAD HEIGHT

Rating:

   Observe the technique in its component parts-

   1.Head action   2. Body action   3. Arm action

   4.Hand action   5. Leg action   6. Feet action

   7. Verbal action   8. Ball Action

Note: IF POSSIBLE NEVER LET A BALL BOUNCE.

"ABOVE THE WAIST" (Training notes):

Type of Serve:
      Beginner   -Underhand tosses (only).
      Intermediate   -Underhand and overhand tosses.
      Advanced   -Instep kick.

Height of Serve:
      Beginner   -About head height.
      Intermediate   -Above head height.
      Advanced   -Vary the height.

Speed of Serve:
      Relative to height of the toss.

Number of Repetitions:
      Beginner   Ten saves   -One minute rest.
      Intermediate Thirty saves   -One minute rest.
      Advanced   Forty five seconds work
                              -One minute rest.

1. Ready Position

2. Reach

3. Catch

4. Secure

IMPORTANT: Confidence building must be the first procedure in teaching "above the waist" saves. The height of the toss can eliminate some of the fears. (Low at first then increase height with technique development).

81

"ABOVE THE WAIST" TRAINING.

Stationary ball. Ball held above waist height by partner.
    -From "Ready Position" use correct technique in taking
      ball from grasp .

Simulated flight. Ball transferred into keepers waiting hands.
    -From "Ready position" use correct technique in collecting
      handed-over ball.

Accurate underhand toss.
    -From "Ready Position" use correct technique in catching
      tossed ball.

TOSS-UP • BOTH HANDS

CATCH SECURE

TOSS-UP • ONE HAND

CATCH SECURE

FULL·SWING TOSS

HALF·SWING TOSS

SIDE·TOSS

SIDE·SWING TOSS

WITH TURNS
TOSS
TURN 90°
CATCH
SECURE

HALF TURN 180°
FULL TURN 360°

VARIATION:

TOSS-UP

CLAP HANDS

CATCH

SECURE

CLAP HANDS BEHIND

TOUCH SHOULDERS

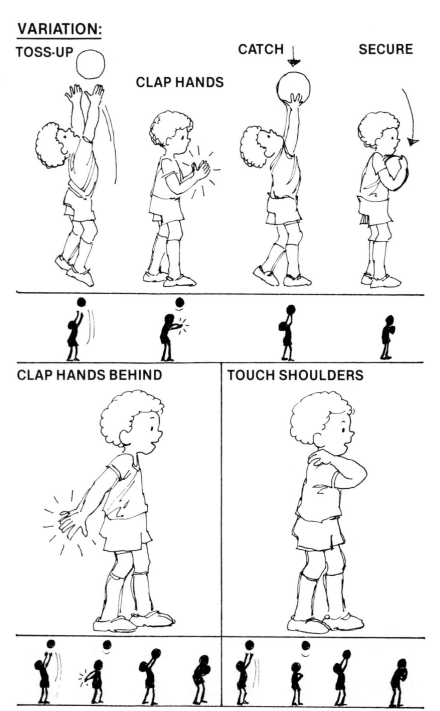

TOUCH BELLY

TOUCH KNEES

TOUCH ANKLES

TOUCH GROUND

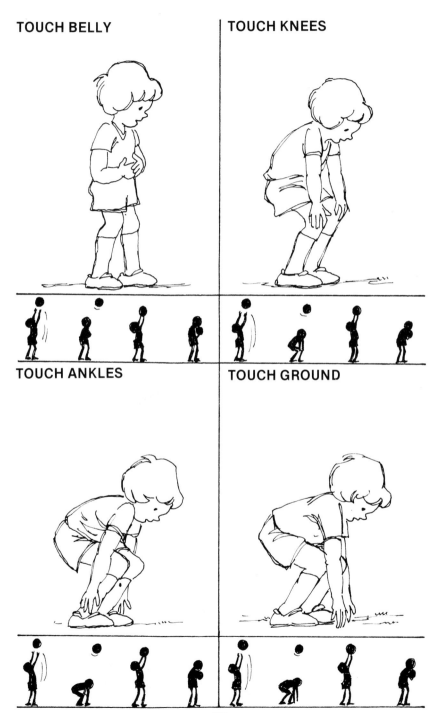

USING A CHALK LINE-ONE FOOT OVER

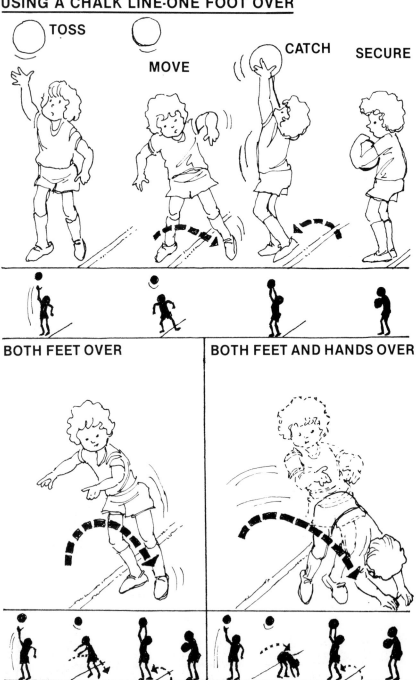

TOSS

MOVE

CATCH

SECURE

BOTH FEET OVER

BOTH FEET AND HANDS OVER

USING AN OBJECT (Example: Cone)

TOSS **TOUCH CONE** **CATCH** **SECURE**

RUN AROUND CONE **JUMP OVER AND BACK**

VARIATIONS of SELF SERVE

KICK-UP

WHILE KNEELING

TOSS-UP•WHILE SITTING

KICK-UP•WHILE SITTING

KNEEL AND UP

PUSH UP

SIT AND UP

BACKWARD ROLL

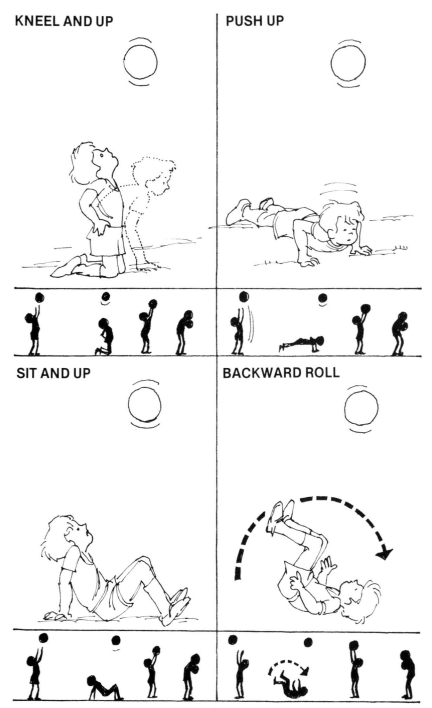

SECURING vs. CATCHING

In addition to catching the ball the **keeper must secure every ball** so that he has total possession.

Two areas of the body are used to prevent the opponent from gaining possession. First, the hands. Second, the back-up portion which may be stomach or chest. Both should be used for **every possession.** From this position the keeper can safely survey the field and release the ball in such a manner that it is to his team's advantage.

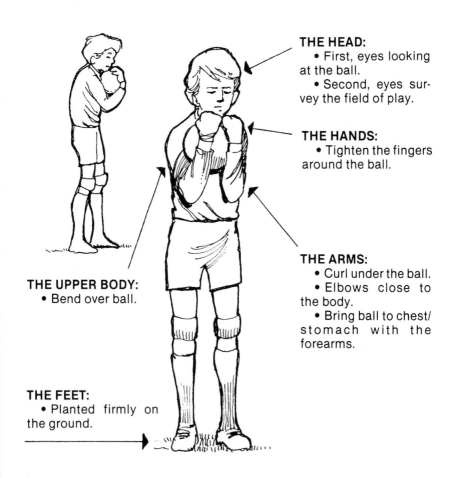

THE HEAD:
• First, eyes looking at the ball.
• Second, eyes survey the field of play.

THE HANDS:
• Tighten the fingers around the ball.

THE ARMS:
• Curl under the ball.
• Elbows close to the body.
• Bring ball to chest/stomach with the forearms.

THE UPPER BODY:
• Bend over ball.

THE FEET:
• Planted firmly on the ground.

SECURING

Common Faults:

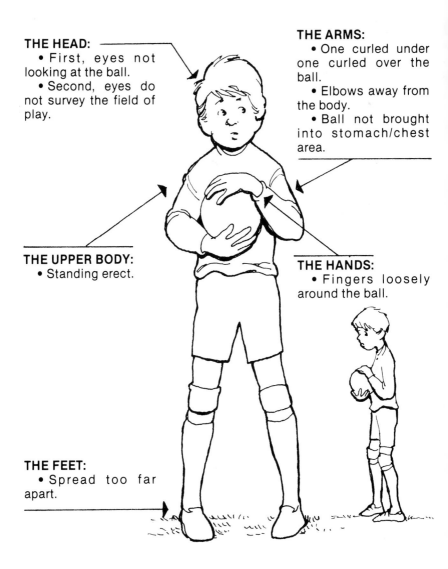

THE HEAD:
- First, eyes not looking at the ball.
- Second, eyes do not survey the field of play.

THE ARMS:
- One curled under one curled over the ball.
- Elbows away from the body.
- Ball not brought into stomach/chest area.

THE UPPER BODY:
- Standing erect.

THE HANDS:
- Fingers loosely around the ball.

THE FEET:
- Spread too far apart.

MOST COMMON: Keeper makes no attempt to "Secure" the ball at all.

DISTRIBUTION:

Bowling

Bowling is a more accurate form of distribution than kicking. Therefore, have the keeper roll the ball to an open teammate. This helps guarantee continued possession of the ball. The bowling ball is favored by the field players since they do not have to concern themselves with controlling a high or bouncing ball.

The action is similar to that of delivering a bowling ball.

1.
HEAD:
• From the "secure" position survey the field of play.

2-3
THE HANDS:
• On the back swing hold ball securely with **both hands.**
• On the forward swing spread the fingers for a more secure hold.

4.
THE ARMS:
• Pendulum motion from back swing to follow-through.

5.
THE UPPER BODY:
• Bent slightly at the waist.

6.
THE LEGS:
• Knees bent to bring ball close to the ground (prevent any kind of bouncing).

SPECIAL NOTES TO KEEPER:
• Release the ball with sufficient speed to reach your teammate.
• Follow your release in case your teammate needs help.
• Be careful in releasing ball on wet or muddy ground because ball may not reach its intended target due to conditions.

BOWLING

Common Faults:

I.
HEAD:
 • Field is not surveyed from "secure" position. **(Usually a catch and kick sequence.)**

2.
HANDS:
 • Ball held by one hand on back swing.
 • Loose grip on forward swing.

3.
THE ARMS:
 • No follow-through on forward swing. (Results in insufficient speed of ball to reach teammate.)

4.
THE UPPER BODY:
 • Erect — leaving ball far from the ground. (Results in bouncing release.)

5.
THE LEGS:
 • Knees stay locked — leaving ball far from the ground. (Results in bouncing release).

6.
THE FEET:
 • Close together. (Results in loss of balance.)

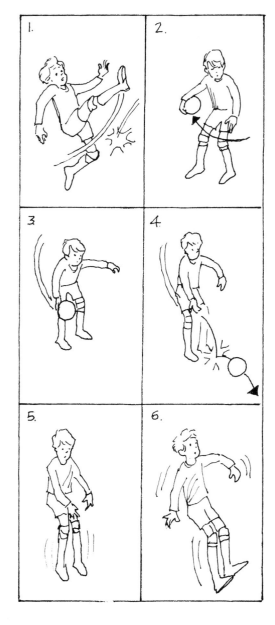

MOST COMMON FAULT: Keeper is not taught "when" and "how" to distribute ball in bowling fashion.

TESTING "BOWLING" DISTRIBUTION

Purpose: To see how proficient keeper is in "Bowling" the ball and what instructions are needed to perfect this skill. Ascertain the distance over which the keeper can accurately distribute the ball.

Suggested Test:
   Ten tries at various targets.

Rating:
   Observe the technique in its component parts—
   1. Secure/Survey   2. Head action   3. Body action
   4. Hand/arm action   5. Leg action   6. Ball action

"BOWLING" NOTES:
PREFERRED AREAS for "Bowling" DISTRIBUTION.

Note to Field Players:
Once your keeper is in this stance you should move into offensive
positions and think "total" offensive soccer.

Note to Keeper:
Direct your players to move forward and spread out.

DISTRIBUTION:

Baseball Throw

To extend the range of delivery but not sacrifice accuracy the goal-keeper can use the "baseball throw". The action is similar to that used by an overhand pitcher in baseball, except the palm and slightly spread fingers cradle the ball. Since fairly large hands are required for palming the ball this technique becomes fairly difficult for young players to handle. However, they should be encouraged to practice this technique by steadying the ball with both hands.

KEY POINTS:

1. From the "secure position" survey the field of play.

2. Bring ball to head height with both hands.

3. Bring ball over the shoulder (cradled in palm—fingers slightly spread).

4. Bring the ball forward, snapping wrist at moment of release and follow through.

5. The flight of the ball should be kept low (without spin), so that the teammate has no difficulty controlling it.

6. Follow your pass in case your teammate needs help or returns ball to you for second distribution.

* Distribute to the sides of the field, avoiding direct counter-attack.

DISTRIBUTION

Punting

The most commonly used, yet most inefficient method of distribution, is punting. Kicking the ball just to get it away from the goal is not good soccer. Maintaining ball possession is good soccer.

Punting—lacks accuracy. Statistics will verify that the majority of punts go to the opponent.

Punting—hinders ball control. The steep drop of the ball can be hard to control by the receiver.

Since ball possession cannot be assured from punting only those keepers who can punt past the midfield should be allowed to punt the ball.

KEY POINTS:

1. From the "Secure Position" survey the field of play.

2. The ball is dropped from the hand opposite of the kicking foot (kicked before touching the ground).

3. Plant foot: Firmly entrenched in ground with maximum body weight on plant foot.

4. On the backswing — bring heel as close to buttocks as possible. (Make toes rigid and lock ankle.)

5. On forwardswing — keep toes rigid and ankle locked.
— snap knee at contact with ball.
— toes move across the body.

6. Plant foot rises.

IMPORTANT: Beginners should not strive for distance but for accuracy and good technique.

"MODERN" TRAINING.
IN YOUR QUEST FOR CREATIVITY KEEP IN MIND THE FOLLOWING NEEDS:

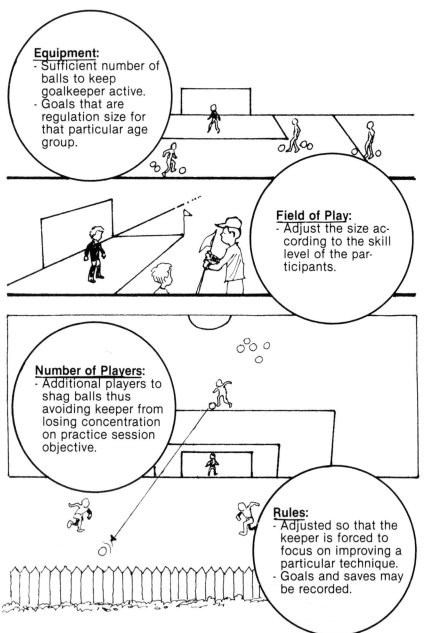

Equipment:
- Sufficient number of balls to keep goalkeeper active.
- Goals that are regulation size for that particular age group.

Field of Play:
- Adjust the size according to the skill level of the participants.

Number of Players:
- Additional players to shag balls thus avoiding keeper from losing concentration on practice session objective.

Rules:
- Adjusted so that the keeper is forced to focus on improving a particular technique.
- Goals and saves may be recorded.

THE MORE COMPREHENSIVE APPROACH TO TRAINING A GOALKEEPER.

It is essential that goalkeepers in practice be given a variety of challenges to improve their overall skills. The traditional method of shooting on the keeper is only a part of good keeper training. The purpose of this section is to go beyond the traditional goalkeeper practice of just taking "shots" at the keeper.

Traditional use of goalmouth:

For more traditional ideas:
FUNdamental SOCCER - PRACTICE, by Karl Dewazien.
pages 54-75.
Fred Feathers Publishing Co. © 1985

Shoot on Goal from Both Sides.

Objective:
- Keeper defends goal from both sides.
- Field players score on keeper.

Number of players:
  One or more stationed on opposite sides of goal.

Rules:
- Shoot from behind shooting line.
- Alternate shooting from one side then the other.
- No shooting stationary balls.

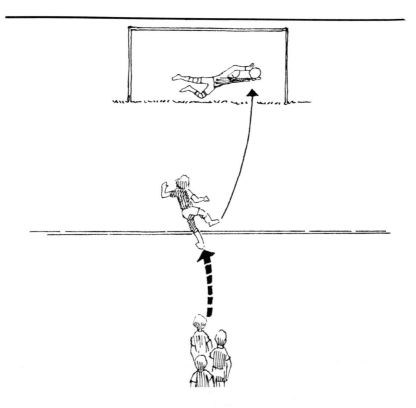

Small Sided Game with Goalmouth in the Middle of the Field.

Objectives:
- Keeper defends goal from both sides.
- Field players score on keeper..

Number of players: Five (5).
  One goalkeeper and two teams of 1 vs. 1 (Minimum)
  up to 6 vs. 6 (maximum).

Rules:
- Follow appropriate laws of the game.
- Shoot from outside "no entry zone".

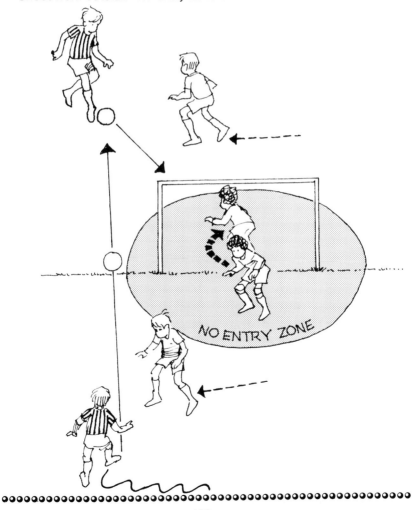

GOALKEEPER vs. GOALKEEPER

Number of Participants: Four (4).
Two keepers and two retrievers.

Objective:
- Defend own goal.

- Score on opponents goal by following commands for hand releases and kicks.

Rules:
- Play begins with one keeper attempting to score on opponent.
- Opposing keeper continues play from point of save. (Note: Scoring attempts must originate from the spot of the save within ones own half of the playing area.)

Game 1: "Bowling" release.

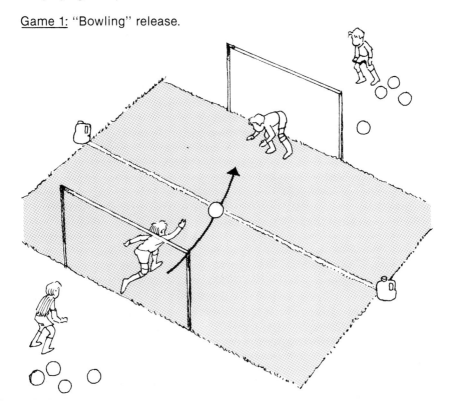

KEEPER vs. KEEPER (Variations)

Game 2: "Baseball throw"

Game 3: Shooting stationary ball.

Game 4: Shooting moving ball.

Game 5: Half-volley shot.

Game 6: Full-volley shot.

Game 7: Specify combination of releases to be used.

Game 8: Allow keeper to use release of his own preference.

SCORING:
- Count number of points scored within a **time limit** or first to reach **21 points.**
- Goal = **2 points.**
- Save resulting in corner kick = **1 point.**

ONE KEEPER vs. ONE KEEPER – plus one neutral shooter.

<u>Objectives</u>:
- Defend own goal.
- Controlled distribution to field player.

<u>Number of players</u>: Five (5).
Two keepers, two retrievers and one neutral field player.

<u>Rules:</u> North keeper serves to field player who shoots on south goal.
- South's keeper continues play by serving to field player from point of save.
- Field player confined to neutral zone (two touch restriction).

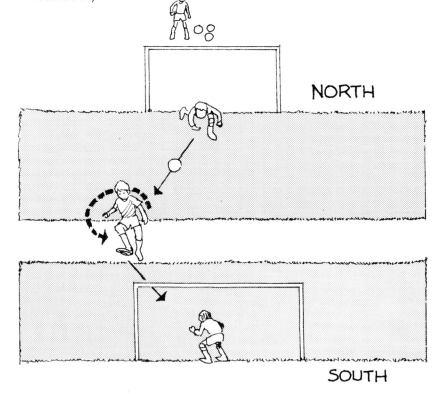

NORTH

SOUTH

ONE KEEPER vs. ONE KEEPER with shooting partner.

<u>Number of players</u>: Six (6).
Two keepers with shooting partner and two retrievers.

<u>Rules</u>: North keeper serves ball to partner who shoots on south goal.
• South keeper serves to his partner from point of save. (Continuous play).

<u>Field players</u>:
• Confined to own half of the playing area.
• Two touch restriction.
• May not interfere with opponent's shot on goal.

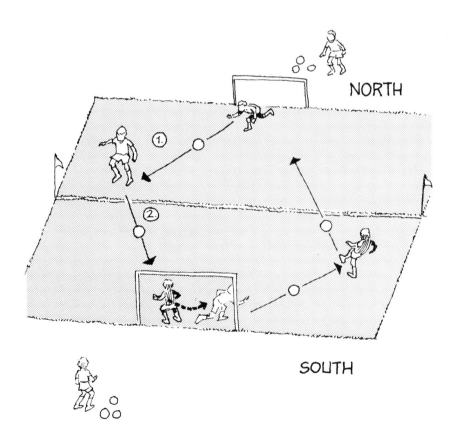

NORTH

SOUTH

VARIATION: Field players interfere with shot on goal —
but only from within their own half of the playing area.

PARALLEL GOALS:

Number of Players: Two keepers with a shooting partner.

Rules:
• Keeper A serves ball to his shooting partner who is opposite keeper B.
• Keeper B, from point of save, serves ball to his field player opposite keeper A.

* Field players may not interfere with keepers releases.

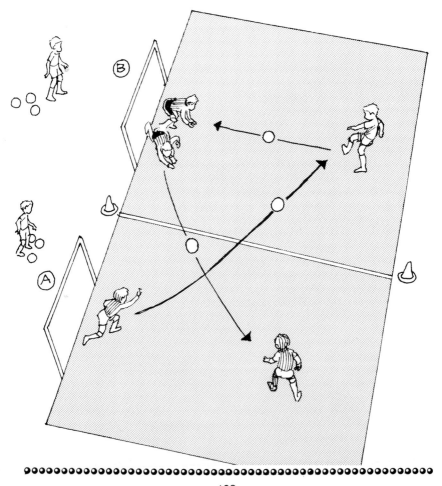

ONE vs. ONE (Small sided game with keepers).

<u>Objective</u>:
• Defend own goal score on the opponent.

<u>Number of Players</u>:
   Four. Two keepers with a partner.

<u>Rules</u>:
• One vs. One keep away "game" by field players.
• Field players attempt to score on opponents goal.
• Field players may not pass ball back to his keeper.

VARIATION: Add more field players and enlarge playing area.

"Modern" Training (Continued)

THREE GOALS

Objective:
• Keeper to defend three goal mouths.
• Field players attempt to score on all three sides.

Number of Players: Three (3).

Keeper plus two or more field players.

Rules:
• Field players may not enter "no entry zone".
• Limit field players to time for getting off shot (Ex: ten seconds or more). or
State time limit after a given signal.

• Keeper may run through the middle for saves.

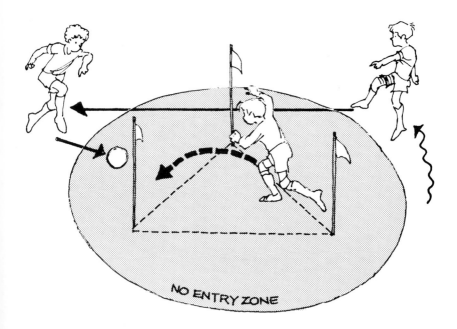

NO ENTRY ZONE

VARIATION: Keeper may not run through the middle for the saves — must **stay outside the goalposts.**

MODIFIED LAWS
UNDER-6 PLAYERS

Follow FIFA Laws of the Game– except for these modifications.

LAWS of the GAME
for Under 6 Players.

LAW 1. FIELD OF PLAY.

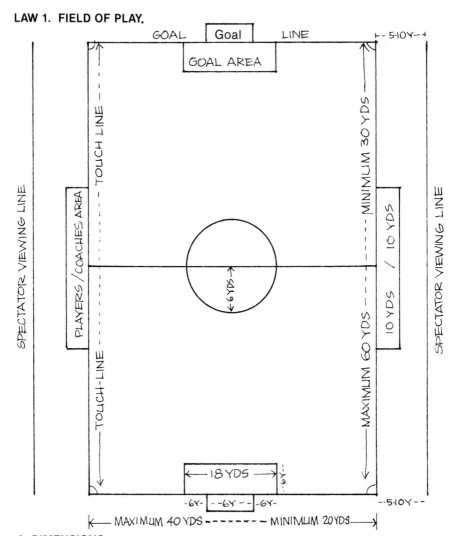

A. DIMENSIONS:
The field of play shall be rectangular. The length shall exceed the width. (See Diagram)

B. MARKINGS:
Distinctive lines from 2-5 inches wide, Halfway line, Center circle, Four corner arcs, Goal area, Players/Coaches Area, Spectator Viewing Line. (See Diagram).

C. THE GOALS:
The goals shall consist of two upright posts six yards apart and equidistant from the corner flags.
Measurements: Six feet high and
               Six yards wide. (Eighteen feet wide).

ALTERNATE FIELD OF PLAY
Using an adult size regulation field, make two youth fields.

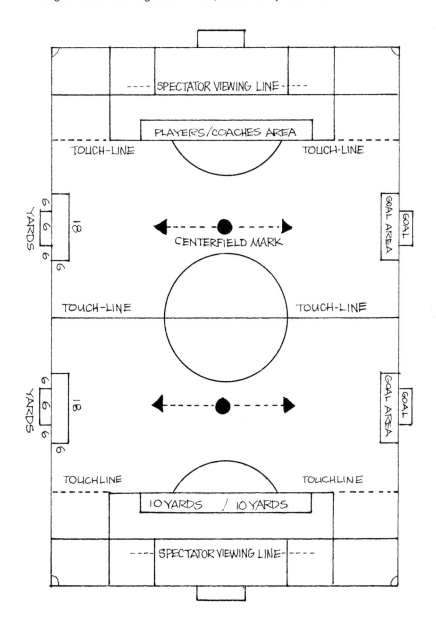

A. DIMENSION
Length: Touchline to opposite touchline of an adult size field.

Width: Half-way line to the penalty area line of an adult size field.

B. MARKINGS
A centerfield mark is recommended in place of the center circle.

LAW 2. THE BALL
Size Three (#3)

LAW 3. NUMBER OF PLAYERS
- Five – No Goalkeeper.
- The maximum number of players on the roster should not exceed nine.
- Playing Time: Each player must participate a minimum of 50% of the total playing time.
- Substitution: During "substitution break" or at half time.
- Recommendation: Teams should be co-ed.

LAW 4. PLAYERS EQUIPMENT
- Jersey or shirt with number on back, shorts, stockings, footwear.

Note: A player shall not wear anything which is dangerous to another player or to himself.

LAW 5. REFEREE
- Shall be encouraged to explain an infraction to the offending player, without undue delay of the game or showing favoritism to either team. Referee should address both teams not an individual while doing so.
- If player continues to use incorrect skill after being advised by referee as to the correct method – allow play to continue but advise by word that error is being overlooked for the good of the game.

LAW 6. LINESMAN
Assist center referee on off-side, ball out of play and follow any instructions given by center referee.

LAW 7. DURATION OF THE GAME
- The game is to be divided into two halves of 15 minutes each.
- The "substitution break" shall be whistled by the referee mid-way through each half.
- Half-time break shall not exceed five minutes.

LAW 8. THE START OF PLAY
- Opponent must be 6 yards from the center mark when kick-off is being taken.

NOTE: The ball is not in play until it travels its own circumference and cannot be touched by kicker a second time until touched by another player.

LAW 9. BALL IN AND OUT PLAY
NOTE: The ball is out of play when it has wholly crossed the goal or touch lines.

LAW 10. METHOD OF SCORING
- The whole of the ball must cross the goal line between the goal posts and under the cross bar.
- The ball cannot be thrown, carried or intentionally propelled by hand or arm over the goal line.

LAW 11. OFF-SIDE
Conform to FIFA laws of the game

LAW 12. FOULS AND MISCONDUCT
- A "foul" is <u>any</u> play which possibly could result in injury.
- The referee should explain all infractions to the offending player in "less than 50" words.

Note: If explanation requires more than "50 words" wait for end of game to do so.

LAW 13. FREE KICKS
Shall be classified under ONE heading — "INDIRECT". This means — a goal may not be scored until the ball has been played or touched by a second player — of either team.

LAW 14. PENALTY KICKS
NO penalty kicks

LAW 15. THROW-IN
One rethrow must be allowed if foul throw occurs.
Referee shall explain fault before rethrow.

LAW 16. GOAL KICK
- Goal kick may be taken from any point inside the goal area - six yard area.
- Opponents must be six yards away from the ball.

LAW 17. CORNER KICK
- May be taken from any point inside the corner arcs.
- Opponents must be six yards away from the ball.

LAW 18. COMMON SENSE
- Do not make rules which will result in boredom, bureaucracy and losing sight of your purpose as an adult.
- Keep no league standings: No publicity.
- <u>Let them have FUN.</u>

MODIFIED LAWS
UNDER·8 PLAYERS

Follow FIFA Laws of the Game— except for these modifications.

LAWS of the GAME
for Under 8 Players.

LAW 1. FIELD OF PLAY

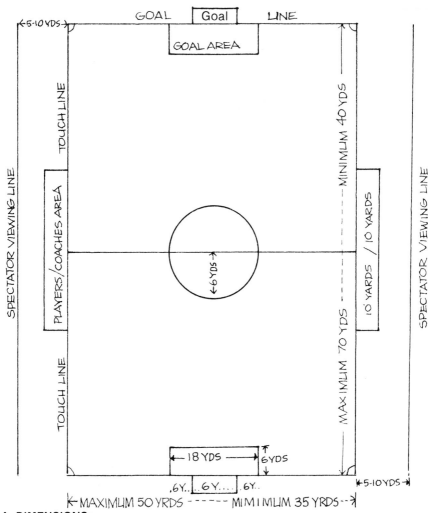

A. DIMENSIONS:
The field of play shall be rectangular. The length shall exceed the width. (See Diagram)

B. MARKINGS:
Distinctive lines from 2-5 inches wide, Halfway line, Center circle, Four corner arcs, Goal area, Players/Coaches Area, Spectator Viewing Line. (See Diagram).

C. THE GOALS:
The goals shall consist of two upright posts six yards apart and equidistant from the corner flags.
Measurements: Six feet high and
Six yards wide. (Eighteen feet wide).

117

ALTERNATE FIELD OF PLAY

Using an adult size regulation field, make two youth fields.

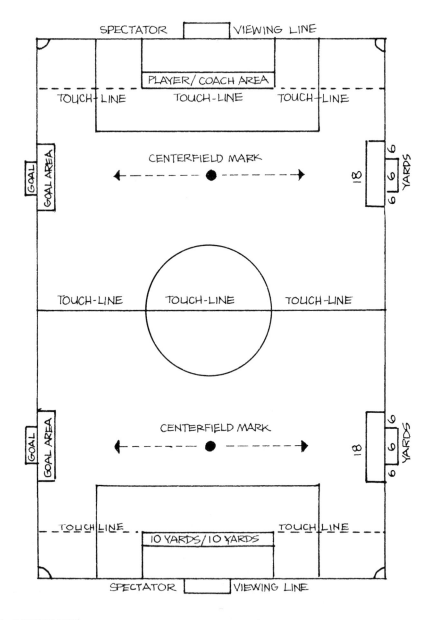

A. DIMENSION

Length: Touchline to opposite touchline of an adult size field.

Width: Half-way line to the Goal area line of an adult size field.

B. MARKINGS

A centerfield mark is recommended in place of the center circle.

LAW 2.   THE BALL
Size Three (#3)

LAW 3.   NUMBER OF PLAYERS
- Seven – One of whom shall be a goalkeeper.
- The maximum number of players on the roster should not exceed eleven.
- Playing Time: Each player must participate a minimum of 50% of the total playing time.
- Substitution: During "substitution break" or at half time.
Recommendation: Teams should be co-ed.

LAW 4.   PLAYERS EQUIPMENT
- Jersey or shirt with number on back, shorts, stockings, footwear.
Note: A player shall not wear anything which is dangerous to another player or to himself.

LAW 5.   REFEREE
- Shall be encouraged to explain an infraction to the offending player, without undue delay of the game or showing favoritism to either team. Referee should address both teams not an individual while doing so.
- If player continues to use incorrect skill after being advised by referee as to the correct method – allow play to continue but advise by word error is being overlooked for the good of the game.

LAW 6.   LINESMAN
Assist center referee on off-side and ball out of play and follow any instructions given by center referee.

LAW 7.   DURATION OF THE GAME
- The game is to be divided into two halves of 20 minutes each.
- The "substitution break" shall be whistled by the referee mid-way through each half.
- Half-time break shall not exceed five minutes.

LAW 8.   THE START OF PLAY
- Opponent must be 6 yards from the center mark when kick-off is being taken.
NOTE: The ball is not in play until it travels it's own circumference and cannot be touched by kicker a second time until touched by another player.

LAW 9.   BALL IN AND OUT PLAY
NOTE: The ball is out of play when it has wholly crossed the goal or touch lines.

LAW 10. METHOD OF SCORING
- The whole of the ball must cross the goal line between the goal posts and under the cross bar.
- The ball cannot be thrown, carried or intentionally propelled by hand or arm over the goal line.

U-8 Laws (Cont.)

LAW 11. OFF-SIDE
Conform to FIFA laws of the game

LAW 12. FOULS AND MISCONDUCT
- A "foul" is <u>any</u> play which possibly could result in injury.
- The referee should explain all infractions to the offending player in "less than 50" words.
Note: If explanation requires more than "50 words", wait for end of game to do so.

LAW 13. FREE KICKS
Shall be classified under ONE heading – "INDIRECT".
This means – a goal may not be scored until the ball has been played or touched by a second player – of either team.

LAW 14. PENALTY KICKS
NO penalty kicks

LAW 15. THROW-IN
- One rethrow must be allowed if foul throw occurs.
- Referee shall explain fault before rethrow.

LAW 16. GOAL KICK
- Goal kick may be taken from any point inside the goal area – six yard area.
- Opponents must be six yards away from the ball.

LAW 17. CORNER KICK
- May be taken from any point inside the corner arcs.
- Opponents must be six yards away from the ball.

LAW 18. COMMON SENSE
- Do not make rules which will result in boredom, bureaucracy and losing sight of your purpose as an adult.
- Keep no league standings: No publicity.
- Let them have FUN.

MODIFIED LAWS
UNDER·10 PLAYERS

Follow FIFA Laws of the Game—
except for these modifications.

LAWS of the GAME
for Under 10 Players.

LAW 1. FIELD OF PLAY

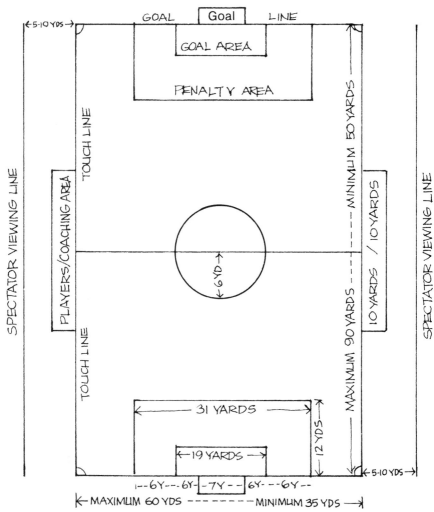

A. DIMENSIONS:
The field of play shall be rectangular. The length shall exceed the width. (See Diagram)

B. MARKINGS:
Distinctive lines from 2-5 inches wide, Halfway line, Center circle, Four corner arcs, Goal area, Penalty area, Players/Coaches Area, Spectator Viewing Line. (See Diagram).

C. THE GOALS:
The goals shall consist of two upright posts six yards apart and equidistant from the corner flags.
Measurements: Seven feet high and
              Seven yards wide. (Twenty one feet wide).

ALTERNATE FIELD OF PLAY

Using an adult size regulation field, make two youth fields.

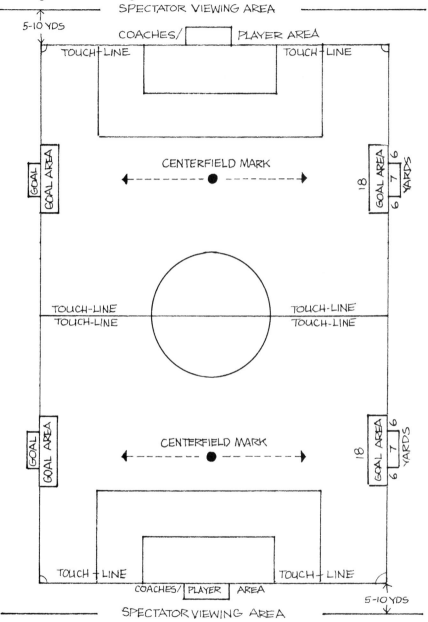

A. DIMENSION

Length: Touchline to opposite touchline of an adult size field.

Width: Half-way line to the Goal area line of an adult size field.

B. MARKINGS

A centerfield mark is recommended in place of the center circle.

LAW 2. THE BALL
Size Four (#4)

LAW 3. NUMBER OF PLAYERS
- Nine – One of whom shall be a goalkeeper.
- The maximum number of players on the roster should not exceed thirteen.
- Playing Time: Each player must participate a minimum of 50% of the total playing time.
- Substitution: During any normal stoppage of the game
Recommendation: Teams should be co-ed.

LAW 4. PLAYERS EQUIPMENT
- Jersey or shirt with number on back, shorts, stockings, footwear.
Note: A player shall not wear anything which is dangerous to another player or to himself.

LAW 5. REFEREE
- Shall be encouraged to explain an infraction to the offending player, without undue delay of the game or showing favoritism to either team. Referee should address both teams not an individual while doing so.
- If player continues to use incorrect skill after being advised by referee as to the correct method – allow play to continue but advise by word error is being overlooked for the good of the game.

LAW 6. LINESMAN
Assist center referee on off-side and ball out of play and follow any instructions given by center referee.

LAW 7. DURATION OF THE GAME
- The game is to be divided into two halves of 25 minutes each.
- Half-time break shall not exceed five minutes.

LAW 8. THE START OF PLAY
- Opponent must be 6 yards from the center mark when kick-off is being taken.
NOTE: The ball is not in play until it travels it's own circumference and cannot be touched by kicker a second time until touched by another player.

LAW 9. BALL IN AND OUT PLAY
NOTE: The ball is out of play when it has wholly crossed the goal or touch lines.

LAW 10. METHOD OF SCORING
- The whole of the ball must cross the goal line between the goal posts and under the cross bar.
- The ball cannot be thrown, carried or intentionally propelled by hand or arm over the goal line.

LAW 11. OFF-SIDE
Conform to FIFA laws of the game

LAW 12. FOULS AND MISCONDUCT
- Resulting in DIRECT FREE KICK:
- Fouls by hand:
  Handling the ball. Holding, Pushing, Striking the opponent (Intentionally).
- Fouls by feet:
  Tripping, Kicking and Jumping at the opponent (Intentionally).
- Fouls by body:
  Charging from Behind, Violent Charging. (Intentionally).
  All other fouls result in INDIRECT FREE KICK.

LAW 13. FREE KICKS
- DIRECT FREE KICK – A goal can be scored direct against the opponent from the point of infraction.
- INDIRECT FREE KICK – A goal may be scored against the opposing team only if the ball is touched by a second player of either team.

LAW 14. PENALTY KICKS
NO penalty kicks.

LAW 15. THROW-IN
- One rethrow must be allowed if foul throw occurs.
  Referee shall explain fault before rethrow.

LAW 16. GOAL KICK
- Goal kick may be taken from any point inside the goal area – six yard area.
  Opponents must be outside of penalty area.

LAW 17. CORNER KICK
- May be taken from any point inside the corner arcs.
  Opponents must be six yards away from the ball.

LAW 18. COMMON SENSE
- Do not make rules which will result in boredom, bureaucracy and losing sight of your purpose as an adult
- Keep no league standings: No publicity.
- Let them have FUN.

REMEMBER:

Keeper may use hands in penalty area.

Keeper wears different color uniform.

Keeper should be proficient in field players skills as well as the unique skills of his position.

Keeper is last line of defense and first line of attack.

Young children often lack the ability to make quick decisions.

The keeper's position calls for mental skills and leadership qualities which many children are starting to develop. Do not rush them!

Teammates have a tendency to place blame on keeper after a goal has been scored -- this must **not** be tolerated.

๏๏

Many youngsters have not learned to accept mistakes--their own or others. "There are two kinds of mistakes -- 'Mistakes' and 'stupid mistakes'. The former should be gently pointed out, the latter with great emphasis".

Vincent Lavery

๏๏

Do not leave keeper in game if he has been scored upon too many times -- or is showing uncertainty in carrying out his role. Do not forget to use words of encouragement as he exits the game.

Rotating players into keeper position will keep their soccer interest alive and improve their understanding of the game and their field performance.

There is no evidence that early specialized training guarantees success.

Specializing too early may discourage the child and cause him to eventually avoid the keeper position. Let his performance/enthusiasm to advance guide you.

The goalkeeping experience must be a rewarding one if it is to be an activity which will continue into adulthood.

๏๏

THEY ARE LEARNERS AND EVERYTHING TAKES TIME TO LEARN.
HAVE FUN. And remember . . .
WHEN A TEAM LOSES ALL ARE RESPONSIBLE.
WHEN A TEAM WINS ALL ARE RESPONSIBLE.

๏๏

BIBLIOGRAPHY

Dewazien, Karl, **FUNdamental Soccer-Practice**, Fred Feathers Publishing Co., © 1985.

Howard, Dick, **The Training of the Goalkeeper**, Canadian National Staff Coach.

Ladislav, **Voetbaltraining**, Eurha Sport, Amsterdam, © 1982.

Machnik, Joe, **So you want to be a Goalkeeper!**, Soccer for Americans, © 1982.

Maher, E. Alan, **Complete Soccer Handbook**, Parker Publishing Co., Inc., © 1983.

Pfeifer, Werner, **Fussball Praxis**, Wurttembergischer Fusballverband, © 1984.

Special thanks to Hans deGraef, Alan E. Maher and Ken Mitchell.